TPM FOR AMERICA

What It Is and Why You Need It

TPM FOR AMERICA

What It Is and Why You Need It

Herbert R. Steinbacher
and
Norma L. Steinbacher

Foreword by
James T. Thompson

Publisher's Message by
Norman Bodek

Productivity Press

Cambridge, Massachusetts   Norwalk, Connecticut

Address all inquiries to:

Productivity Press
P.O. Box 3007
Cambridge, Massachusetts 02140
(617) 497-5146 (telephone)
(617) 868-3524 (telefax)

Cover design by Gary Ragaglia
Printed and bound by Maple-Vail Book Manufacturing Group
Printed in the United States of America on acid-free paper

Library of Congress Cataloging-in-Publication Data

Steinbacher, Herbert R.
    TPM for America : what it is and why you need it / Herbert R. Steinbacher and Norma L. Steinbacher ; publisher's message by Norman Bodek.
      p.   cm.
    Includes bibliographical references and index.
    ISBN 1-56327-044-7
    1. Plant maintenance -- United States -- Management.   I. Steinbacher, Norma L.   II. Title.
TS192.S7614   1993
658.2'02--dc20

                  92-31388
                  CIP

93 94 10 9 8 7 6 5 4 3 2

Dedicated to
James Andrew
and His Grandmother

Contents

Publisher's Message   ix
Foreword   xiii
Acknowledgments   xvii
Introduction   xix

PART I: Why TPM?   **1**

1   Who's Minding the Store? Wake Up, America!   3
2   The Change Process: It's Not Easy   9
3   Background: How We Got Where We Are   13
4   Our Current Status: Getting Clobbered   19
5   Defining TPM: What It Is — and Isn't   25
6   The Value of TPM: What It Can Do for You   35

PART II: Getting Started   **45**

7   Understanding Change: The People Problem   47
8   Three Stages of Change: Initiation, Implementation,
     and Institutionalization   59
9   Maintenance Prevention: "No Problem!"   67
10   Predictive Maintenance: A Stitch in Time   79

11   Corrective Maintenance: If It Ain't Broke,
        Fix It Anyway   87
12   Preventive Maintenance: Do or Die   93
13   Autonomous Maintenance: Abolishing the Fiefdoms   97

PART III: Conclusions   **103**

14   Progress: Who Is Doing TPM?   105
15   Case Studies: TPM In Action   109
16   Consequences: So What If We Don't Do It?   117
17   Action Plan: Entering the TPM Race   123

Resources   **127**
Glossary   **131**
Notes   **135**
About the Authors   **141**
Index   **143**

Publisher's Message

As an executive or manager in an American manufacturing enterprise, you are undoubtedly aware of the problems that can get in the way of your company's ability to serve its customers.

- Defective products lead to losses, missed deadlines, or complaints
- Machines break down too often and take too long to fix, making it impossible to achieve just-in-time or one-piece flow production
- New equipment doesn't operate at its rated speed
- A grimy, dark plant presents an unimpressive face to visitors and hides problems of all kinds
- The work environment leaves employees demoralized and uninvolved in improving the business

No company in this condition can operate successfully, particularly if it is trying to do just-in-time production. Rational corporate leaders might try to solve what they perceive as separate aspects of the problem. They might try for more employee involvement by installing suggestion boxes or starting improvement groups. They might tackle quality problems by having their managers trained in statistical process control or mistake-proofing techniques. They might hire more maintenance technicians to fix the machines faster or more janitors to try to keep the place looking neater.

Unfortunately, these solutions generally fall short of the mark. As the introduction to *TPM for America* points out, equipment maintenance is the very foundation of industry, and total productive maintenance (TPM) is the basis on which all other world-class manufacturing strategies rest. What is distinctive about the TPM approach is that it merges total employee involvement, quality improvement, and state-of-the-art maintenance technology to improve the equipment capacity utilization of a plant and the quality of the product. TPM is a set of initiatives that can be tailored to any manufacturing situation, promoting support for equipment availability companywide, not just in the maintenance department.

TPM for America devotes a full chapter to each of the five main elements of a TPM program:

- maintenance prevention
- predictive maintenance
- corrective maintenance
- preventive maintenance
- autonomous maintenance activities by equipment operators.

Companies need to implement all five elements or a combination of several to achieve the optimum benefit from TPM.

Maintenance prevention is the design or selection of equipment that will not break down easily and is easy to access when maintenance or repair is required. *Predictive maintenance* involves the use of historical breakdown and repair information in conjunction with observation or the use of sensing equipment so that repairs or parts replacement can be done at the optimum time before a machine breaks down or produces defects. *Corrective maintenance*, sometimes called *improvement maintenance,* includes activities to modify and upgrade equipment so that problems will not recur. *Preventive maintenance,* already well established in many U.S. companies, uses periodic routine maintenance to prevent major problems. Last but not least, *autonomous maintenance activities* involve equipment operators in keeping the machines running smoothly, through daily cleaning and inspection as well as training to recognize early signs of trouble and make simple repairs. As you might expect, the operator involvement aspect of TPM requires a change in attitudes in the workplace. Operators can no longer think, "I run it, you fix it." Nor can the maintenance staff think that they are the only ones who need to know how the machines work. TPM requires everyone in the company to recognize the importance of equipment availability and work cooperatively to sustain it. Herbert and Norma Steinbacher wrote *TPM for America* specifically to reach the audience that most needs to understand the TPM story—the executive leaders of American industry. TPM is a major initiative with far-reaching benefits for every company. Although much of the actual maintenance work is done at the shop-floor level, it is imperative that TPM have the full support of company leaders and decision makers. The Steinbachers bring together years of experience in the fields of maintenance management and educational counseling to demonstrate the critical need for TPM and for the training and investment in your people that go with it.

As this book stresses, support for TPM means not only verbal and visible encouragement in as many ways as possible, but also consistent funding for the training required to solve equipment problems, make improvements, or predict and prevent breakdowns. Operators need to be educated about basic equipment mechanics and how to recognize when things aren't right; maintenance staff often find themselves in a new teaching role. Far from putting skilled mechanics out of work, training operators to do routine inspection and simple repairs frees the maintenance staff to work on equipment improvement, advise equipment builders on how to put together maintenance friendly machines, and learn new technologies involved in predictive maintenance. Top management needs to continually emphasize these benefits of TPM for the continuing development of its employees. In terms of human resources alone, TPM is an investment in the company's future that will be repaid many times.

Productivity has been actively promoting TPM-related education since 1988 because we believe it is the single most important manufacturing improvement strategy to emerge from Japan. Whether or not you are attempting just-in-time production, without a TPM program your company is losing huge sums due to equipment downtime and cost of quality. If you *are* trying to do JIT, consider TPM the basic foundation for keeping your lines running and delivering to customers on time. We hope that this book will inspire you to learn more about how TPM could be significant to your company. Truly, you cannot afford *not* to know about it.

I would like to express my appreciation to the Steinbachers for permitting us to publish this book. Thanks also to Bruce Graham for his early editorial work with the authors and to Karen Jones for developmental editing; to Dorothy Lohmann for editorial management, with Laura St. Clair (word processing and proofreading); to Gayle Joyce for production management and typesetting; to Northwind Editorial Services for indexing; and to Gary Ragaglia for cover design.

Norman Bodek
President
Productivity, Inc.

Foreword

Approximately two and a half years ago, Magnavox Operations embarked on a very aggressive journey intended to improve all aspects of our performance. Many different initiatives support this journey toward improved quality, all based on the foundation of continuous process improvement. Absolutely essential to the success of these initiatives is the concept of employee involvement and empowerment. TPM is an excellent example of this.

At Magnavox, through some long-standing efforts such as VECI (Valued Employees Contributing Ideas) and MAGIEC Circles (our version of the quality circle concept) and more recent initiatives such as JIT/QC and TPM, we are actively permitting and encouraging all of our people to participate in the management of our business. The manager's role is not only to support these efforts, but sometimes just to stay out of the way and allow them occur. My feelings about TPM, therefore, are far less important than the opinions of our manufacturing associates/team members, maintenance technicians, and others actively involved with TPM. I believe these are the opinions and feelings that truly count. It is apparent that, through TPM, our employees are gaining a much greater appreciation for the importance of equipment cleanliness and maintenance and are truly taking ownership and experiencing greater pride with respect to their equipment and their jobs.

I am an extremely strong supporter of TPM because it meshes perfectly with our continuous improvement theme and our emphasis on teamwork, education, and communication. As Herb and Norma Steinbacher show in *TPM for America*, upper management commitment to these elements is critical to the success of TPM. Continuous improvement implies a dissatisfaction with the status quo — with the way equipment runs and often with the way people relate to each other at work. If corporate leadership is satisfied, the company will never attain world-class status.

In many plants, as in ours, the cultural shift to a teamwork environment is the most difficult of any of the changes brought by TPM. We were fortunate in that virtually all of our previous improvement initiatives were heavily team oriented so that we were reasonably well prepared for the TPM culture. The Steinbachers rightly focus on this critical issue throughout the book. It would be difficult to overemphasize the importance of top management's visible commitment on this point. The attitude change and dissolution of barriers that TPM requires on the shop floor must begin with an executive team that not only says the right things, but also demonstrates the willingness to actually let people exercise much greater control of their working environment. At Magnavox, it's okay to try and fail — that's how our people learn. People can achieve remarkable results when you give them the training and authority to do their best — and make it clear that you will not tolerate a return to the old "I run it, you fix it" pattern of factory life.

The Steinbachers underscore the importance of training at all levels: training operators to clean and inspect their equipment, spot early signs of trouble, and make simple repairs; training maintenance staff in advanced preventive, predictive, and improvement techniques; training everyone in the team-work skills required to reach the goal of optimum equipment effectiveness.

The cases shared in *TPM for America* describe the progress of TPM implementation at Harley-Davidson, Allen-Bradley, Eaton, and TechniStar. Our experience at Magnavox has also followed a gratifying course of development. It is interesting to note that although initially our TPM teams concentrated primarily on cleanliness and maintaining equipment performance, the TPM focus has now evolved to the actual enhancement of equipment performance. The impact of this focus on improved product quality and cost-effective operation should be obvious.

Interestingly, the initial expectation was that autonomous maintenance activities by the manufacturing team members and associates would decrease the maintenance technicians' work loads. In fact, the opposite has occurred in many cases, due to the manufacturing team members'/associates' greater knowledge concerning their equipment, and their desire to continually enhance its performance. In a TPM operation, the maintenance technicians become teachers and mentors. They spend a greater proportion of their "hands-on" time using their specialized technical skills to optimize equipment performance rather than just keeping it running. The logical result is a more effective utilization of their time and skills and far greater job satisfaction for all those involved.

We at Magnavox see TPM as a crucial element in our ability to be competitive now and in the future. *TPM for America* should persuade you to pursue TPM as a strategy for your own company's long-term success.

James T. Thompson
Senior Vice President and Director of Operations
Magnavox Electronic Systems Company

Acknowledgments

Writing this book has been a unique experience for us because it has been a completely joint effort. It is a blending of two very different perspectives that are more complementary than we realized when this project began. We have been able to combine our talents and our backgrounds in ways that have presented us with a broader view of the challenges facing manufacturing and how to prepare workers for the future.

We might never have reached our goal, however, had it not been for the help and encouragement of some very special people. An undertaking of this nature is much easier with support from family and friends, and we are grateful to all of ours, especially Mom, who helped with some of the early editing, and our son, James, who offered encouragement throughout the process.

A special thanks is due to those who participated in making this book a reality. Norman Bodek's enthusiasm and understanding of the need for TPM was the match that ignited the flame. Connie Dyer believed in our efforts and gave the manuscript to Bruce Graham, who made excellent suggestions for improvement. Finally, Karen Jones assumed editorial responsibilities and brought the book to print.

Steve Armstead and Ron Quigley reviewed the manuscript with a critical eye to both content and mechanics. Their ongoing, longtime involvement as champions of TPM well qualified them to pass judgment, and we are grateful for their expertise.

Those who provided information about their companies for inclusion in this manuscript impressed us with their cooperation and dedication. Thank you, Jeanne Boyd, Miles Snyder, and Jim Steger. Thank you, Wayne Vaughn and Dave Bjork. Your time and willing involvement were invaluable.

Introduction

A new way of thinking and acting is beginning to emerge in U.S. manufacturing. Maintenance, an activity long ignored in the executive suite, is coming into the limelight as managers discover its importance. What was once a dirty word is recognized today as an activity essential to the well-being of the entire company.

American manufacturers regrettably have not supported maintenance — the very foundation of industry — while demanding ever-greater performance from it. We do not accord the respect to the technician who repairs a machine that we give to the one who designs it. Yet, the work of the mechanic who ensures all engines on an airplane are working properly is as important as the aircraft's pilot or designer.

Maintenance is an art and a science. As we recognize this, we are finally beginning to refocus priorities and restructure organizations to meet ever-increasing global competition. At last we are beginning to realize that total productive maintenance (TPM) is the foundation on which all other world-class manufacturing strategies must rest. Without TPM, neither just-in-time nor total quality management exist — at best they are only dreams. Without TPM, total employee involvement is incomplete. The proper operation of equipment is as essential to a successful production setting as employee involvement.

The high attendance at the first TPM conference in the United States, held in 1990, proves that many U.S. industries are eager to take advantage of the profitable returns of TPM. Maintenance managers, supervisors, and engineers, seeking information about how TPM can work for them, looked to others in similar positions for support and successful strategies. But the battle is still being waged, and the war has not been won. While so many were taking an active interest in TPM, those essential to the success of TPM were absent.

Where were the CEOs and those in charge of operations? Ron Quigley, director of facilities and plant engineering for the Industrial Control Group of Allen-Bradley, Co. Inc. (a Rockwell International company), voiced a familiar sentiment: "If your vice president of operations isn't tuned in to TPM, it will be difficult to contain future maintenance costs. It requires management's full support for the program — up front."

Guiding a company through the dangerous shoals of the global marketplace is no easy task. Those in charge must have greater skill and understanding of *all* phases of their business than ever before. Maintenance technicians can no longer remain the "unsung heroes" of industry. Survival demands a change in the old adage that those who understand the need for change lack the power to accomplish it, and those who have the power lack the vision. Those who have the power to speed the development of TPM strategies still don't understand that TPM is essential for survival.

Companies with proactive executive leaders who have removed barriers and begun developing a TPM strategy are finding benefits beyond their expectations. Maintenance costs are higher than senior managers (even those in charge of finances) realize, accounting for 15 to 40 percent of total product cost. A reduction in maintenance costs is equivalent to increasing profits from sales more than threefold. Additionally, employees experience greater job satisfaction and customers are more satisfied with the product when quality is built in.

Development of an appropriate TPM strategy is the most important as well as the most challenging undertaking for companies of the 1990s, and beyond. Whenever change is introduced, it brings anxiety and stress. It upsets the status quo, creating a fluidity within the corporate culture that is very unsettling. Despite the agony, change must occur for the individual or the corporation to grow.

Employees working in the area of maintenance already know the importance of their jobs. They can generate support for change that involves machine operators in autonomous maintenance and other aspects of TPM. They can share information with their supervisors, but they cannot carry TPM beyond that awareness level without senior management's support. Application of TPM can occur only when those in authority pave the way. The CEO who places more importance on shipping products than on avoiding defects will prevail over the maintenance manager who wishes to stop production because of a faulty production machine.

A CEO's support is also essential in analyzing and evaluating the strategies being implemented. Since improvements are always possible and mistakes inevitable, workers must feel free to make mistakes as well as to present new ideas. A change, especially a major one, often leaves people tired and ready to remain at a new status quo. Any new suggestion made on the heels of change may meet with resistance, making workers hesitant to present another new idea. Also, suggestions may be good, but workers may not make them if the need for change is not immediately clear to others. We've learned that some must hear an idea at least three times — first for immediate rejection, second for consideration, and finally for acceptance.

Since TPM embodies a major cultural change, it affects the entire corporation and has the greatest impact on plant culture.

As TPM gains momentum on the plant floor, its effects will be realized in the quality and costs of goods produced and in changing expectations about the quality of products purchased. Changes in the way we work demand new attitudes toward education and training. There is a rapidly expanding interface between training and education that is reaching down to the elementary-school level. Companies are providing time for employees to volunteer in the schools, to share information about their work and to train students on the most up-to-date equipment and teach them about current work practices. Courses in technology, including just-in-time and other world-class approaches, are beginning to appear at the middle-school level. Industry is helping to create future employees who have a basic understanding of global economics and the purpose of world-class strategies, including TPM.

Our goal is not to explain the "nuts and bolts" of how to achieve faster setups, establish predictive maintenance, or develop training programs. Seiichi Nakajima, Keith Mobley, Terry Wireman, and others have written on those subjects. Our purpose is to point out the rewards awaiting you as a company leader and to provide some guidance so that you might avoid the pitfalls inherent in such an undertaking. If this book contributes in some small way to the reawakening of our manufacturing "tiger" — our industrial core that has been complacently giving away our markets to those alert enough to take advantage of our shortsighted napping — we will have accomplished our task.

PART I

Why TPM?

1

Who's Minding the Store? Wake Up, America!

Total productive maintenance: What is it? Who needs it? Why bother? If you don't know, your company is either already in trouble or is headed in that direction.

Many often confuse TPM with preventive maintenance, computerized maintenance management systems, or a variety of other maintenance programs or strategies. Our definition includes all the strategies needed to sustain a healthy maintenance organization. The following five components are necessary for a true TPM strategy:

1. *Maintenance Prevention:* designing or selecting equipment that will run with minimal maintenance and is easy to service when necessary.
2. *Predictive Maintenance:* determining the life expectancy of components in order to replace them at the optimum time.
3. *Corrective Maintenance:* improving the performance of existing equipment or adapting new equipment to the manufacturing environment.
4. *Preventive Maintenance:* using scheduled or planned maintenance to ensure the continuous, smooth operation of equipment.

5. *Autonomous Maintenance:* involving production employees in the total machine maintenance process.

While emphasis varies according to the industry, these five
components are essential to TPM. Few companies have a thoroughly developed TPM strategy in all areas. Although some of
these strategies might be given cursory attention, autonomous
maintenance is foundational to TPM. No strategy is workable
without the active involvement of employees.

A SLEEPING TIGER

For the past 25 years, there have been warnings of impend-
ing problems in U.S. manufacturing. We, as consumers and as
leaders of the American manufacturing industry, have failed to
prepare for the onslaught of technical advances that are developing at exponential rates. We currently face major economic
and social changes equivalent to the force that rocked the world
at the beginning of World War II. If the attack on Pearl Harbor
awakened a sleeping tiger, the heady experience of winning the
war generated overconfidence or downright cockiness and a
subsequent lackadaisical attitude that has contributed to our un-
doing. The major changes ahead of us, though centered in the
manufacturing environment, will have far-reaching impacts.

Worldwide political and economic changes are forcing us
to look at new ways of doing business since competition in all
markets is greater than ever before. Our manufacturing industries are in trouble on several fronts. Competition, coupled with
a willingness to abandon markets, has made U.S. industry vul-
nerable to global pressures of unparalleled magnitude. The need
for change in our manufacturing industries has crept in so insid-
iously that markets were lost before companies realized they
were in danger.

The U.S. manufacturing industry is in a major mess.
Though we may be part of the manufacturing environment, as
individuals, we have neglected to study the impact on our own

industries of the growing number of quality foreign products available for our consumption. Most consumers want the best quality for the lowest price. Until we in the manufacturing environment realize that quality is important and attainable only by constant effort, we are going to fall further behind our competitors. Getting back on track will take dedication, skill, perseverance, and hard work far beyond that required to win a war against others, for we have refused to recognize that *we* are the greatest danger to ourselves.

THE COST OF QUALITY

To date, most of us in the industry have skirted the issues, hoping the problems confronting us weren't all that bad, or that, like the flu, they would go away eventually. We have refused to delve too deeply for fear we might find that something is required of us personally. We would rather believe our competitors, our government, our educational institutions, our employees, and even our friends and family owe us, than accept the fact that we might be the ones who owe them.

As we recognize the need for change, we must be willing to share what we learn, and above all we must be willing to apply what we learn. We cannot be so naive as to assume that attending a seminar or reading a book will provide us with all the answers. Because technology is continuing to expand and new competitors are continuing to appear, our only hope for survival is to continually improve — faster than anyone else!

And as soon as improvement is under way in one area, we must look for another area that needs attention. If we've addressed concerns about total quality management, it is probably time to focus on just-in-time or total employee involvement. Chances are, however, that little thought has been given to total productive maintenance, which is potentially one of the most profitable approaches we can consider. Since maintenance is not directly related to any given product, we tend to overlook its per-item cost, which is (depending on the industry) *between 15 and 40 percent of total product cost.*[1] Decreasing costs in this area provides an automatic return of bottom-line profits. This advantage can no longer be ignored; we must assume that other companies have already begun using this potential savings to improve their competitive edge.

WHY CHANGE?

Any company choosing to do business in the twenty-first century will most likely fail if all of its employees do not recognize that methods of the mid- to late-twentieth century are no longer effective. Companies that intend to *be* world class must *think* and *act* world class. As senior management, we must focus on global markets and new ways of doing business if our industries are to survive. We can no longer approach change at a leisurely rate, as if it were a smorgasbord, from which we could pick and choose only those aspects that are most appealing to us. We must use all applicable strategies available to us, or none will have lasting impact.

Simply put, change must occur throughout organizations, from management and its way of thinking to financial planning and outlook to hourly workers and their concerns. Attitudes and ways of working must change, from the CEO to the most recently hired employee. Employees at every level must realize that their failure to produce will bankrupt the company. They must change old nonproductive habits or their jobs will soon cease to exist.

With the explosion in technology, change is happening in many arenas at once, bombarding us continually from all sides. We have no time to assimilate one change before we are in the midst of several more. Our new constant is continual change, which may result in "data overload." Some of us will be able to reset our parameters, while others will succumb to "system shutdown." Those who do shut down, refusing to change, must not be allowed to undermine the change process.

Those of us who do recognize the need for change will be frustrated to the point of ulcers, depression, anxiety, anger, rebellion, and upset. At times, we will be convinced that our efforts are useless. Why would anyone put themselves through such agony? The answer can be summed up in one word: survival. We will do it for the same reason a person undergoes open-heart surgery: Do it or die. If we don't work to become world class and our competition does, we'll be out of business. The companies that have provided the paychecks we depend on will no longer exist.

You say that your company has no competition, so what's the big deal? That's today. Tomorrow may be another story.

2

The Change Process:
It's Not Easy

Change! What does it mean to you? Is it good or bad, needless or necessary, profitable or a waste of time? It may be any or all of those things. Whatever else it is, it is uncomfortable; it forces us into new ways of thinking and doing things. How we respond when confronted with the need for change depends on how it is presented to us and how we perceive it in relation to our own lives. If we initiate the change, we react differently than if it is forced on us. Change is easier to deal with when it affects us only as individuals, because if the world around us seems more constant, we are more able to maintain some sense of status quo. When change involves an entire society, as in war or economic depression, the upheaval is more upsetting to all areas of our lives.

How we as managers and individuals approach changes will determine our success or failure, both economically and politically. If we as a society choose to ignore the need for change, we will become entrenched in insular attitudes. An isolationist outlook will also cost our manufacturing industry dearly. We can no longer ignore the marketplace demands for quality goods and services at a reasonable price.

SATISFACTION AND SUCCESS

We cannot compete with those willing and able to meet — and exceed — customers' demands unless we are ready to do likewise. Indeed, the importance of delighting our customers is gaining worldwide prominence. The Japanese have proved that quality and customer satisfaction can be achieved profitably by adopting quality improvement and preventive maintenance strategies that were initially developed in the United States. Why should it be so difficult to re-adopt that which was ours in the first place?

Impetus for change comes from many sources. For the individual, it could result from a decision to continue one's formal education or to get a promotion or transfer. For a manufacturing company, the incentive may come from declining profits, market saturation, or a new competitor. In other cases, several forces may combine at once, leading to new insights and paths of endeavor.

THE CHANGE PROCESS

Change may affect one individual involved in several different situations or it may affect several individuals involved in a single project. In either circumstance, motivation may be very different for each individual; however, the process by which change occurs is essentially the same.

Michael Fullan,[1] of the Ontario Institute for Studies in Education, has recognized the similarities in the change process. In his research into organizational change, he discovered that factors involving change fall into three stages: initiation, implementation, and institutionalization. This is true in industry as well as in education.

THE NEED FOR VISION

To initiate change, a high-profile *need*, like TPM, must be presented. Because any movement away from the status quo is unsettling, initiating change, however small, creates fear and anxiety. Moreover, people will always be at different stages of accepting change and will require varying degrees of psychological and technical support as they learn new skills through practice and feedback. It is also easy to lose sight of the objectives in daily activity. Therefore, a strong advocate is necessary to keep both the need and the desired outcome visible. Without a continuing sense of urgency and a vision of what things will be, the comfort of the status quo is much too enticing.

Once the need for change is recognized, those who see it must devise a means of meeting it so satisfactorily that the need no longer exists. It must become a habit that is completely embedded in all activities and attitudes. Only then will the change become institutionalized.

ORCHESTRATING CHANGE

In general, the process behind carrying out change is often overlooked. However, if the change has widespread magnitude (like developing world-class strategies), this process cannot be ignored. It must be carefully orchestrated by those leading the change. The people in charge must be fully aware of what is happening. A lack of sensitivity to the acceptance level of the other parties involved can undermine any accomplishments.

THE HUMAN COMPONENT OF TPM

If machines are the heart of TPM, employees are the arteries and veins that carry the product from inception to completion. Since TPM requires a significant change in the behavior of all employees, we will constantly refer to the change process when dealing with employee attitudes toward change.

The most difficult message for many to accept is that TPM involves more than machines and maintenance personnel. Machine operators have a vital role, as do engineers. Anyone involved with the business unit for a given product has a role in some aspect of TPM, including the secretary who must accurately and quickly produce records, letters, and memos, and the custodian who changes the light bulbs. Everyone must realize that each individual's work contributes to product cost as well as to company profits and that the amount available for raises or bonuses directly relates to efficiency in completing assigned tasks. Thus, everyone must recognize the need for change at the individual level as well as at the departmental and corporate level.

3

Background:
How We Got Where We Are

When we began researching the topic in 1988, total productive maintenance was a new term. Richard Schonberger had given it some attention in his book, *World Class Manufacturing*, but little else was in print. What was TPM? How did it differ from preventive maintenance? What were its components? We discussed these issues daily and prepared a research questionnaire to help us gauge what was being done. When the questionnaire was ready for distribution, there was still no book on the subject of TPM printed in English.

By the time we began work on this book, Seiichi Nakajima's books outlining Japan's TPM strategies, *Introduction to TPM* and *TPM: Development Program*, were available in English. *Training For TPM* by Nachi-Fujikoshi has been added to the list, as well as books on various components of TPM. Since the late 1980s, articles related to TPM have appeared with increasing regularity in trade magazines. TPM seminars are being conducted by several companies, and the National Award for Maintenance Management Excellence has been established for large companies. Despite all this attention, little information is available about how to successfully implement TPM in U.S. companies.

THE SHAPE OF A NATION

Whenever something new appears, it is natural to want to know where it comes from and why it exists. We want to know the sources of disease and its cures. We want to know the backgrounds of our heroes, politicians, and leaders, as well as the history of our financial and industrial institutions. Such information better enables us to evaluate these people or institutions. When discussing the origins of TPM, saying that the strategy comes from Japan is just as unsatisfying and perhaps even more erroneous than saying our legal system comes from Great Britain.

The history of modern manufacturing is intimately intertwined with the growth and development of our nation; it has shaped us, just as we have shaped it. Japan, on the other hand, has used its cultural history to shape its industrial development in a manner totally impossible in the United States, where we are forever trying out new methods and ways of doing business. For example, General Electric originated the term TPM more than 40 years ago. Since then, it has been ignored, for the most part, in the United States. American companies looked at other means of generating quick profits, while Japan chose to embrace the concept as a means for producing quality goods at low cost.

ACCELERATING PRODUCTION

Manufacturing history in the United States began in the seventeenth century when farm families crafted products using hand tools. This home crafting developed into small community shops, leading slowly to commercialized industry. Since the early society was agrarian, problems of speed and quantity were immaterial. Though impetus came from Eli Whitney's musket production, industrialization did not become significant until after the Civil War. It was not until after World War I that manufacturing technology gained international status.

World War II further accelerated production technology as the machine tool industry continued to provide quality products at low cost while paying high wages to employees. As war generated new demands, industry met the challenge through continuous improvement. One of the earliest examples was at the General Motors Saginaw Steering Gear Division, which exceeded the production requirements set for the Browning .30-caliber machine gun by 100 times and cut the cost of each gun from $667 to $144.[1]

THE TIGER NAPS AGAIN

Many companies involved in the production of tanks, jeeps, guns, ships, and aircraft accomplished feats similar to Saginaw's. Cost minimizing, essential in a wartime economy, demanded systematic attention to product design and all-around plant efficiency. At the end of the war, the momentum carried industry into new arenas of technology and productivity as the reconstruction of devastated countries became the focus of attention. The United States could afford to be generous and show others how to do things. After the bombing of Pearl Harbor, the Japanese ambassador to the United States said he feared his country had awakened a sleeping tiger. The events of World War II proved the accuracy of his concern. At the end of the war, however, the tiger, having proved its prowess, was satisfied with its place in the international scheme of things and went back to sleep.

As countries recovered from the wartime destruction, they adopted the cost-minimizing strategies of U.S. industries. At the same time, a military-industrial-scientific collaboration was set in motion in the United States. Government contracts for military and space projects were assigned on a cost-plus basis. Because profits were already built in, it was no longer essential to focus on cost-cutting while improving quality. This led to declining productivity rates in the United States while productivity rates in Germany and Japan were improving. Between 1965 and 1975, the average annual rise in productivity rates per labor-hour in manufacturing were 10 percent in Japan, 5 percent in Germany, and 2 percent in the U.S. By 1980, the U.S. average annual productivity rate declined to $-.5$ percent.[2]

According to manufacturing researchers Robert Hayes and Steven Wheelwright,[3] rapid economic growth after World War II coupled with profit-centered organizations and a shortage of well-trained general managers caused the decline of manufacturing productivity in the United States. The low prewar birthrate helped create an abundance of positions for the available personnel, leading to rapid promotions in burgeoning industries. Many of these new managers had interrupted their education due to the war. They often moved from job to job and company to company before they were able to gain in-depth experience or to note the consequences of their managerial decisions. Companies had little commitment to their managers because of the rapid turnover rate and, in turn, received little loyalty or long-term experience from them.

CHANGING PRIORITIES

Senior managers became more concerned with their decision-making power than with productivity as their tenure was often too short to bring any major productive goal to its conclusion. Short-term profits became more important than long-term goals. This has led to the de-industrialization of U.S. companies, many of which are putting more money in outside investments than in renovating their factories.[4]

This de-emphasis of manufacturing technology is supported by the view that we are becoming a service-oriented society based on knowledge rather than production and has led to the deskilling of American workers. Factories outside of the United States have replaced 25 percent of our technicians, engineers, and blue-collar workers.

FALLING BEHIND

It has become evident in recent years that the United States needs to be competitive in manufacturing technologies and that U.S. companies can succeed in international markets by refocusing on cost-minimizing practices. Failure to do so will result in business deterioration similar to that in the United Kingdom, where, in 1959, senior managers rejected suggestions about ways to improve productivity. We are already dependent on imports for 25 percent of our machine tools. Only 2 percent of numerically controlled (NC) machines are now manufactured in the United States, although they were developed at the Massachusetts Institute of Technology in the late 1950s under the auspices of the U.S. Air Force.[5]

Government selection of designs led to tools priced beyond the reach of U.S. firms. Ultimately, Western Europe and Japan took over the market for small and mid-sized firms. Computer NC and direct NC equipment overtook NC machines by 1980, before the use of NC equipment had become widespread. By 1985, the new generation of machines and technologies were also obsolete and being replaced by flexible manufacturing systems capable of handling small lot sizes and rapidly changing product designs.[6]

What have we been doing about the problem? So far, not much. Stupidity, stubbornness, laziness: call it what you will. Our individual and corporate egos have found it easier to blame someone else than to accept responsibility for our actions and inaction. We do not want to endure the discomfort of change. Yet without change, we will relinquish our precious product markets and our livelihood to those more willing to work for them.

4

Our Current Status: Getting Clobbered

Mirror, mirror, what do I see?
Is the image you project really me?
Is it the surface or truly the whole —
Revealing the essence of my soul?

Manufacturing expert Thomas Gunn[1] has said that as a society, we lack the image of ourselves as a global competitor and that this perception has led to the decline of our industrial institutions. Hayes and Wheelwright[2] also recognized the general perception around the world that American workers and managers do not care about quality. They further concluded that competing successfully in international markets requires a willingness to customize the product to meet individual market needs.

GIVING AWAY THE GOOSE

Like Jack, of beanstalk fame, U.S. industrial leaders found a goose that laid golden eggs — manufacturing equipment that creates products. Shortsightedly, we have valued the eggs more than the goose. The failure of American manufacturers to recognize and meet the domestic need for smaller, more economical cars led to market dominance by foreign automobile manufacturers. Though some recognized the problem, most industries continued to do business as usual, and the problem did not go away. In 1987, Tom Peters wrote:

> The United States is getting clobbered in steel, autos, semiconductors, construction, and financial services alike. . . . Koreans prefer Japanese over American suppliers by a wide margin. . . . For the most part, the quality of made in America goods and services is questionable; perhaps "stinks" is often a more accurate word.[3]

Lester Thurow[4] honed in on some of the reasons, noting that American industry cannot produce goods at the price and quality achieved abroad because of the lack of an adequately trained work force, too little savings and investment, and the failure to see production as a central task. The result is that U.S. companies experience more downtime for repairs, more shoddy products, more assembly line defects, and more service calls.

Despite these pervasive problems, U.S. industries have been slow to improve production processes. With a few notable exceptions like Corning, with its development of optical waveguides, American firms are less willing than companies in many other nations to invest in new equipment that promotes safety or improves product quality, in worker training, or in research and development, especially in low R&D-intense industries. In 1985, for example, GE stopped production of microwave ovens at its new factory. Though the market was booming at the time, the company did not wish to invest in the high engineering costs necessary to compete in this market.[5]

GOOSE HUNTING

In the past decade, a renewed importance has been placed on process improvement technology in our economy. Some companies have used these new approaches to compete very successfully in the international marketplace. Much has been written about the success of Japanese companies that learned management techniques for producing low-cost, high-quality goods from W.E. Deming and others.

As American companies begin seeking answers to the problems besetting them, Deming[6] has indicated some direction for finding solutions. He suggests that problems are self-inflicted by a corporate leadership that has turned away from its manufacturing purpose and has instead focused on dividends and good performance on the stock market. In pointing to management as a source of difficulty, Deming also identified management as vital to recovery. Management must be committed to the long-term goal of manufacturing quality products at low cost. Management must also be committed to innovation, a stable production system that paces strategy according to resources, and adherence to assumptions underlying strategic choices (as long as they hold), and must be willing to change direction if conditions render the original assumptions obsolete.[7]

Unfortunately, there are no simple solutions in the quest for recognition as a world-class manufacturer. Programs such as lifetime employment (guaranteeing workers employment until retirement), which at first seems to account for part of Japanese manufacturing success, do not impact all industries in Japan nor are they available to all workers. Lifetime employment is available to less than half of the Japanese work force; it is not available to temporary employees or women and carries a mandatory retirement age of 55 for men working in the large companies that offer the benefit.[8]

Success goes far beyond factors such as individual culture, automation, and wage rates. As Harley-Davidson, Inc., chairman Vaughn Beals has said, "When we recognized that our competitors were simply managing their operations better than we were, we were on the road to success."[9] As managers, we must be willing to admit that problems result from what we are doing and failing to do, not because of what others are doing to us. Only then do we have a chance of rediscovering our golden goose.

Finding the goose may not be as difficult as it may seem. The trick in finding anything is to look in the right place. How often have you said, "It was staring me in the face!" So it is with our manufacturing problems. The answers are not somewhere in outer space but within our own organizations.

BECOMING WORLD CLASS

Although there are no quick fixes, certain themes recur among successful companies around the world. These themes are the cornerstones of what is becoming known as world-class manufacturing (WCM). It is a concept of continuous improvement. The key strategies of WCM are total quality management, just-in-time, total employee involvement, and total productive maintenance. Each must be given equal attention for our industries to succeed successful.

Though no one company has completely implemented all of these strategies, a growing number of companies have begun the effort. Could the tiger be reawakening?

The figure on page 23 helps illustrate the interdependence of the key strategies of WCM. Total employee involvement is at the top and permeates each of the other strategies; total productive maintenance provides the base that keeps the other strategies in place. The removal of any segment destroys the square, just as removing any of the components destroys WCM.

When industries first recognized the need for change and began looking for ways to become more profitable, quality control was identified first as an area in need of improvement. Richard Schonberger wrote in 1982 that quality improvement is everyone's responsibility and should be built in at each step of the production process. Just-in-time is a strategy to reduce waste; one of its basic principles is to produce only the amount of product needed to fill current orders, thereby reducing inventory. Since products are produced on a demand basis, raw materials also should be delivered on demand. In addition, JIT deals with

A World-Class Manufacturing Model

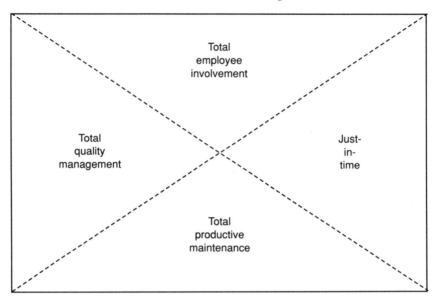

eliminating waste at all levels of the organization and stresses the importance of *value-added* operations. Total employee involvement is necessary to the success of all aspects of WCM and should be instituted throughout the organization. Unlike the single-issue approach of TQM or JIT, total employee involvement is the foundation for quality, cost, and delivery issues that directly affect customers.

This is also true for TPM, which has received much less attention than the other components of world-class manufacturing. In the past, articles and books on manufacturing process improvement generally devoted few words to the importance of maintenance. The topic is receiving more attention as its importance is increasingly recognized.

Unfortunately for industry, this lack of attention to a vital area has gone beyond that of literary oversight. The means of keeping production machinery operable has been ignored throughout history. Far too often people have considered maintenance as menial and insignificant in relation to production.

Schonberger also recognized the importance of maintenance,[10] but did not label it as a major component of WCM until 1986. In 1982, he considered "housekeeping" important for quality control, safety, and pride because it improved work habits, quality and care of equipment, and the facility. He pointed out that Japanese workers were trained to do routine checks on equipment and to fix some breakdowns. Preventive maintenance, he said, was important to keep equipment running smoothly and to prevent production lines from shutting down unexpectedly. By 1986, Schonberger devoted more attention to TPM, which he identified as one of the four components of WCM. He stated that TPM is necessary to "maintain the equipment so often and so thoroughly that it hardly ever breaks down, jams, or misperforms during a production run."[11] The goal of TPM is to "make present equipment completely reliable so it can do a job in a uniform, dependable cycle time with no question about quality."[12] TPM is indispensable for world-class manufacturing, because when equipment is working properly, costs drop, productivity rises, and defects and lead times are reduced.

5

Defining TPM:
What It Is — and Isn't

Total productive maintenance is a support strategy for improving all aspects of manufacturing; it must be in place for total quality management and just-in-time to be effective. TPM involves the following:

1. *Maintenance prevention* in the design and selection of new equipment
2. *Predictive maintenance* to determine the life expectancy of components
3. *Corrective maintenance* to improve equipment performance
4. *Preventive maintenance* on a scheduled basis to ensure the continuous smooth operation of equipment
5. *Autonomous maintenance* to involve production employees in the total machine maintenance process

The importance of TPM is understandable when you consider that production machine reliability must be consistently high to support throughput and that TPM is the only strategy that specifically provides such support. According to Masaaki Imai, "In this era of slower economic growth, better equipment utilization [is] as important as manpower and system improvements."[1] Equipment reliability controls process predictability. Thus, as Richard Lubben notes, just-in-time "forces a company to go into total productive maintenance to develop an environment of predictability from the point of view of the equipment."[2]

IS IT REALLY CHEAPER?

Some aspects of TPM have long been part of most maintenance programs. They have not, as yet, been incorporated into a synergistic system. This is necessary for greatest effectiveness. For example, maintenance prevention — the design or selection of easy-to-maintain equipment has often been overlooked in concern for initial costs. Lower-priced equipment is favored over a more expensive item that might have lower maintenance costs over its lifetime.

This problem is common to many aspects of our lives, such as in choosing a heating and cooling mechanism for a new house. A heat pump unit might seem like an inexpensive option up front. Home builders, like plant managers, do not always consider the cost of operating the unit over time, the maintenance costs, or the cost of changeover when the unit needs to be replaced.

Maintenance prevention involves selecting or creating equipment designs that incorporate ideas and features to reduce overall repair requirements over the life of the machine. Saving $20,000 on the purchase price is no savings if repair costs are five times higher than those of a higher-priced machine that has been designed with maintenance prevention in mind.

THE MANUFACTURER'S CRYSTAL BALL

Predictive maintenance is the planned replacement of parts that are known through historical data to have a certain service life. Predictive maintenance is essential to a smooth production flow because it enables you to replace parts before they fail and to avoid disrupting production schedules. Predictive maintenance can be accomplished only when workers understand its importance and are committed to providing the data necessary to make predictions.

Statistical process control and computerized maintenance management are necessary tools for predictive maintenance. Workers must collect and store data for comparative purposes. The cost of recording information will be recovered many times over since the time lost for planned maintenance is less costly than breakdown maintenance. Workers must be convinced that the information they provide is vital, and they must be willing to learn the procedures for using the tools to record data. The company that actively supports TPM should either train people in using computers or assign someone who already has the skills to operate a computerized maintenance management system.

DEBUGGING AND ALTERATIONS

Corrective maintenance gives manufacturing engineers the ability to use historical data in problem solving and modification techniques to improve operating reliability of machines. Corrective maintenance is based on input from production, maintenance (including technicians and machine-shop personnel), quality services, engineering services, and purchasing.

Corrective maintenance is vital to TPM and must be part of the process to continuously improve machine performance and reliability; this includes more than equipment modification. Modification and updating of manuals and prints is also essential. Changes must be clearly documented so everyone who works or will work with the machine has the information necessary to solve problems, make decisions, and operate the machine at optimal levels.

How wonderful it would be if every machine operated perfectly as soon as it was installed. In reality, however, the machine usually doesn't run, the design manuals are incomplete, and the design engineer is busy on another high-priority project and can't be bothered with debugging this one. The task is usually left to the maintenance technician, who should have been involved in the initial design, but probably wasn't. Correction is more expensive than prevention — just ask any car manufacturer involved in a recall.

At times, corrections are impossible. Some new car models are designed so that changing spark plugs is impossible without a lift or special tools. In the past, this was a routine maintenance operation often done by the car owner and requiring very little time. Now it is a major and more costly task usually left to the garage mechanics. Once access to the spark plugs is designed into a car, it cannot be changed. Recognizing problems such as this in the design stage could result in a bit of maintenance prevention, which would please many customers.

Since Allen-Bradley Co., Inc. (a Rockwell International company) designs and builds its own production equipment, the company has addressed the problems of corrective maintenance by having designated "development mechanics" help with costing out designs, beginning in the maintenance prevention phase. Maintenance personnel are cross-functional and may transfer from one area to another based on skill and education.

Allen-Bradley also has "machine repair mechanics," who repair and maintain the equipment to manufacturers' specifications, and "machine builders," who make parts and assemble them according to blueprints. The development mechanics create prototype machines and special equipment using pneumatics, hydraulics, and/or robotics. Continuing education in approved coursework (which varies according to classification) is a requirement for maintaining classification and pay grades.

Not all corrections result from poor design. Sometimes modifications are needed for specific applications. Most of us have alterations made when buying clothing, if we want an exact fit. Fine-tuning to smooth out an operation is also a form of corrective maintenance. Corrective maintenance should be the primary focus with new equipment since making corrections early in the life of a machine reduces total life-cycle costs.

IF IT AIN'T BROKE, FIX IT ANYWAY

Preventive maintenance is probably the most commonly used element of TPM. Mechanics oil, grease, check, and adjust machine parts, replace worn parts when required, and check performance on a variety of equipment, just as homeowners re-paint siding, replace worn carpet and broken windows, and fix leaky faucets. Failure to make needed repairs leads to property devaluation, deterioration, and even danger. Similar financial losses apply to production machines and companies.

Harley-Davidson Motor Company greatly improved its preventive maintenance strategy with a lubrication program that reduced lubrication-related calls for the maintenance department from two or three a week to approximately one a month. Further cost reductions result from improving the identification and control of lubricants and enforcing lubrication activities.

The interrelationship of TPM strategies is evident in the Harley-Davidson program. Predictive maintenance techniques are used to identify which equipment needs lubrication and to determine the frequency of lubrication. Involving maintenance personnel, machine operators, and production supervisors in the program is autonomous maintenance in action. Developing clear, simple written instructions and a thorough training program have contributed significantly to achieving a world-class lubrication program.

PEOPLE MAKE IT HAPPEN

Autonomous maintenance, the fifth component of TPM, in-volves production employees in cleaning, inspection, lubrica-tion, adjustments, and problem solving. Someone who drives a car daily will notice a faulty front-end alignment much sooner than the mechanic who sees the car once or twice a year; likewise the operator who works with a machine every day will be the first to notice fluctuations in performance. Similarly, skill levels of drivers can range from filling the tank when fuel is low to something as complicated as relining the brakes. Skill levels of machine operators are equally varied.

We've often expected our employees to operate as robots, checking their brains when they punch the time clock and retrieving them at the end of the workday. By allowing machine operators greater autonomy in their work environment, they can prove the extent of their capabilities. During a plant visit, we asked a worker how she felt about making adjustments to production machines in addition to doing routine cleaning and inspections. No problem, she responded; after all, she'd rebuilt the carburetor on her car engine over the weekend, and it performed perfectly.

Machine operators such as that woman are prime examples of what autonomous maintenance is all about. If people can manage other important aspects of their lives, developing budgets, balancing finances, making daily decisions, and interacting with family members, they should be able to apply these same skills in the workplace.

Not everyone, of course, is capable of performing more technical tasks. Employees who are willing to change but are incapable of meeting the new higher standards of performance can be transferred to other jobs compatible with their capabilities. Anyone who refuses retraining or an appropriate transfer does not have a place in a world-class organization.

People must be willing to work to their potential, and they must also be aware of their limitations. There is a difference between using untapped potential and assuming potential that does not really exist. Accepting responsibility beyond one's capabilities can be as devastating to the individual and the company as failing to perform to one's fullest ability.

Because machine operators have a unique knowledge of their equipment, they should be included in all phases of TPM.

They have a different perspective on what is needed in a new machine, as does the maintenance mechanic, the design engineer, and the company controller. Operators must provide much of the data for predictive maintenance and corrective maintenance through their logs on stoppages, routine maintenance, and breakdowns. They may also be the first to recognize the need for a machine modification by zeroing in on abnormalities in machine operation that could indicate a potential problem.

> Until we believe that the expert in any particular job is most often the person performing it, we shall forever limit the potential of that person. . . . Nobody knows more about how to operate a machine, maximize its output, improve its quality, optimize the material flow, and keep it operating efficiently than do the machine operators and maintenance people responsible for it.[3]

OOPS! WE GOOFED!

Though TPM is an effective strategy, it is not without its pitfalls. One of the major dangers is that as companies work to become world class, they often change manufacturing objectives without changing the method for measuring manufacturing performance.

Manufacturers must develop operating measures designed to provide information for the specific needs of an organization, based on such nonfinancial controls as quality, delivery, scrap, inventory, and equipment maintenance. Such measurements are often referred to as "local performance measurements." Measuring uptime and downtime and reviewing repair records, for instance, can provide a better economic understanding of true maintenance costs. Viewing equipment simply as a fixed asset or measuring machine effectiveness and utilization through traditional methods is no longer relevant.

TPM is a tool for more meaningful accounting procedures as well as an improved work flow.

TPM MEANS BENEFITS GALORE

In addition to the financial benefits of reduced downtime, improved quality, and increased equipment reliability, TPM will have other effects on the organization. Operator training allows employees more control over the work, thereby increasing worker satisfaction and a sense of involvement and ownership in the equipment. Maintenance personnel are able to deal with more difficult problems as their expertise increases. They have the ability to concentrate on bottlenecks that have the potential for disrupting throughput.

Although no one will necessarily be out of work, as the TPM strategy gains momentum, maintenance departments may require fewer technicians. For instance, when TPM was introduced at Topy Industries' Ayase Works in Japan,[4] the work of the maintenance department was transformed. As machine operators took over routine tasks, maintenance technicians were trained to do more sophisticated maintenance, including equipment diagnostics; they also gave training to machine operators. In three years, the 600 Ayase workers identified 9,000 trouble spots on machines, installed 1,467 limit switches, reduced breakdowns that caused short line stops from 1,000 to 200 per month, and slowed oil leakage from 16,000 to 3,000 liters per month. Labor productivity was up 32 percent and breakdowns were down 81 percent. Tool replacement time was reduced 50 to 70 percent, cost of defectives was down 55 percent, inventory-turnover ratio was up 50 percent, and the equipment operating ratio was up 11 percent.

Performing routine preventive maintenance allows for less deterioration of equipment, which can make it more economical to simply upgrade old equipment when changes are needed. Records provide necessary data to determine the feasibility of upgrading a machine or replacing it. Finding the root cause of an equipment problem is more cost-efficient than assigning personnel to babysit a finicky machine.

MAKING IT HAPPEN

As Harley-Davidson[5] discovered, total commitment is essential for total productive maintenance as well as for total quality management, just-in-time, and total employee involvement. During initial phases of TPM, it is possible for maintenance to become overextended due to problems discovered during routine inspections of equipment. A well-developed training program for machine operators will help you avoid the pitfalls of downtime, high overtime, and excessive work backlog. The training program should explain the rationale for change, teach new skills, provide an understanding of the strategy, and encourage input from employees.

In considering the expense of TPM, Schonberger[6] points out the necessity for considering the *value added by TPM*, especially in allowing for scheduled downtime. A machine that is running and producing bad product is more costly than if it were idle. "High average downtime is costly, but it is high downtime variability and bad quality that can be fatal."[7] Thus, scheduling time for preventive maintenance at the end of each shift may be more cost effective than operating machines three shifts per day. Preventive maintenance cannot be sacrificed for production schedules. If it is, production schedules will ultimately suffer during expensive breakdown maintenance.

TPM can be implemented only with the support of management and all employees associated with production. Everyone in the company must be personally convinced of the need for TPM and must develop a sense of ownership in the strategy. By accepting the logic of TPM as common sense, it will be possible to develop consensus for applying TPM in areas of management, logistics, and behavior.[8] A thorough understanding of the strategy and its purpose will help to overcome difficulties inherent when a new method is adopted.

World-class manufacturing companies have come to recognize the importance of TPM and are beginning to use it to combine their total quality management and just-in-time strategies with total employee involvement and equipment reliability. Companies seeking to attain world-class status would do well to make TPM an integral part of new policies when tailoring strategies to fit their unique needs. "A world-class competitor with the ability to continually improve is virtually impossible to catch."[9] Though TPM is not a quick fix, maintenance, according to expert Keith Mobley, "can do more to improve profitability than any other part of the corporate structure."[10]

6

The Value of TPM:
What It Can Do For You

What can TPM do for a company? Is it worth the time, trauma, and turmoil inherent in any major change? We are not talking about a change in the way a machine is installed or lubricated but a change in the way people think, act, and interact throughout an organization. Change of this magnitude must provide incredible payoffs to be worth the investment. TPM generates such payoffs, and if approached properly, it will assure the support necessary for cost-effective production.

IT'S A SECRET

The benefits of TPM can only be estimated, since they have never been fully documented. We discovered early in our research that many companies place their TPM efforts in the category of proprietary information. If competitors know how well or what a company is doing, they have an advantage in planning their own strategies. The need to maintain a competitive edge is understandable, but this confidentiality makes it difficult for researchers to determine what is worthwhile and what is not. We urge companies to adapt a more collegial position in this regard, guided by common sense about how much information to share.

GET THE MOST FOR YOUR MONEY

Machines that are broken or that run inefficiently are a drain on profits. Unfortunately, we have become such a "throw-away" society that we don't look carefully enough at life-cycle costing. Paying attention to the cost of equipment and its life-time maintenance is an essential component in determining product cost. Backup equipment can be as costly as breakdown time; even when it isn't, keeping the regular machinery operating properly is more cost efficient. Most of us do not have an extra car in case the one we normally drive breaks down since the cost of the extra car as well as registration, insurance, up-keep, and storage make it highly impractical. We expect the vehicle we drive to run properly, with minimal breakdowns, as long as we do the routine maintenance and servicing established by the manufacturer.

IS TPM REALLY IMPORTANT?

Most companies committed to performing in the world-class arena recognize the importance of TPM. We surveyed 179 organizations in 1988[1], including companies in two categories: Those that Schonberger[2] identified as "world class" — having made a fivefold or better improvement in productivity — and those listed in the *Directory of Colorado Manufacturers* that employed more than 200 people. (With the exception of one Colorado plant that did not respond to the survey, there was no overlap between the two primary categories.) Of those responding to the survey, the companies identified as world class are most apt to recognize the need for TPM. Also, the need for TPM was seen as important most often by large companies. Eighty-eight percent of the surveyed companies identified as world class and employing over 500 people already had implemented some aspects of TPM; the rest of the larger world-class companies did not respond. Half of the smaller companies said the nature of their business was such that they did not need TPM, while 38 percent reported having some form of TPM strategy in place. Of the other companies, over 20 percent were unfamiliar with the term or the strategy. Less than one-third of all the companies asked had any form of TPM strategy in place at the time of the survey, and 10 percent of the companies that answered the survey did not respond to the TPM questions. It seems that those who aspire to world-class status would be wise to emulate those who have achieved it.

PLUS AND MINUS

In the course of our research, we asked those companies that claimed to use TPM strategies to list the benefits or problems they had encountered during the implementation or after. The responses reflected their enthusiasm for TPM even in the problem areas. *Improved machine performance* was mentioned most often as a benefit. This was followed in order by

- reduction in costs
- improved employee relations and involvement
- customer satisfaction
- improvements in problem solving
- improved scheduling and reduced paperwork

The more deeply a company was involved in TPM, the greater the satisfaction with the strategy. Because of the sensitive nature of issues related to financial status, it was determined that an indirect assessment of the relationship between operating costs and TPM would best serve the purposes of the study. Among world-class companies, 48 percent of the benefits noted were related to improvements in machine performance and 23 percent directly addressed cost reductions and control. One respondent noted *no breakdowns since adopting TPM*. The table on page 38 shows company responses with regard to downtime after use of TPM or other world-class strategies.

This research is compatible with that of others who have also noted dramatic improvements in machine performance and

Changes in Machine Downtime Among Companies
(Percentage of companies reporting downtime changes
grouped according to strategies in use)

	WC TPM	WC No TPM	CO WC-TPM	CO WC-OTH	CO No WC
Downtime Reduced	50	17	50	15	43
No Change	10	50	33	62	43
Downtime Increase	10	—	17	—	—
Data Not Available	30	33	—	23	14

WC/TPM: Company was identified as world class and reported using TPM.

WC/No TPM: Company was identified as world class and reported that TPM was not used.

CO/WC-TPM: Company was located in Colorado and identified as world class and using TPM.

CO/WC-OTH: Company was located in Colorado and identified as using other world class strategies, but not TPM.

CO/No WC: Company was located in Colorado and was using no world class strategies.

reduced costs. Keith Mobley, who concentrates primarily on the predictive aspect of TPM, found that production output could be increased 50 percent by improving existing production processes.[3] Since maintenance contributes an average of 28 percent to the total cost of finished goods, any reductions in maintenance expenses will have a dramatic effect on product costs and company profits. A 2 percent reduction in costs is equivalent to a 7.5 percent gain in sales[4], which makes these figures even more attractive.

There are also difficulties in implementing TPM, most of which are not directly related to the benefits. Many of these relate to ingrained attitudes or management approaches that are incompatible with TPM activities:

- production management reluctance to release equipment for preventive maintenance
- machine operator attitudes ("It's not my job," or "Only I can coax good product from this machine")
- lack of financial support (a high-level "attitude" problem)
- scheduling issues
- start-up costs
- maintenance personnel attitudes (fear of job loss or extra work)

CAUSE AND EFFECT

According to Richard Schonberger, TPM's goal is to make equipment so reliable that it *always* functions properly, thereby assuring quality.[5] Fewer defects and reduced lead times increase productivity and decrease costs. Increased productivity in conjunction with reduced costs is the heart of world-class manufacturing. This makes good sense because breakdown maintenance is three times as costly as preventive maintenance.[6]

Maintenance improvement expert Tom Stevens notes that maintenance has a significant impact on quality, cost, and scheduling and is a strategic tool for improving a company's competitive edge. He points out that "where continuous maintenance improvement is introduced for the first time, plants may see initial effectiveness increases of 30 to 50 percent, followed by subsequent smaller yearly increases, all with little or no capital investment."[7]

Just-in-time requires properly maintained equipment to meet production schedules. At one company, for example, a machine that produced an expensive item broke down, and replacement took six months. Problems resulting from this one breakdown resulted in hundreds of thousands of dollars in lost revenue in just a few weeks. In addition, employees lost wages and morale plummeted. This story can be told many times over.

Another company discovered that a plastics injection mold was out of tolerance because of wear, resulting in a loss of one-third of its production capacity for over a week. In cases such as these, disaster might have been avoided through appropriate TPM strategies.

Through predictive maintenance, American Cyanamid's Westwego, Louisiana, plant was able to avert a gearbox failure. Although the gearbox could have been backed up by a steam turbine, it would have increased costs by $26,000 per month. Recognizing abnormal signs of wear made it possible to make temporary repairs until new gears made to more rigid specifications could be installed in a scheduled shutdown environment without disrupting production.[8]

In our research we also found that data related to the results of TPM were often intermingled with other world-class strategies. Where a company has instituted more than one world-class component, good results may be gained, but it is not always possible to show exactly what generated the improvement. However, a comparison of downtime among the world-class and Colorado companies surveyed indicates a positive correlation between the use of TPM strategies and a reduction in machine downtime (which improves productivity). Consultant Ira Magaziner and columnist Mark Patinkin have concluded that the only way to compete successfully with low-wage countries is through improved productivity.[9] Thus, elimination of machine malfunction downtime is vital.

HELP FOR HUMAN RESOURCES

In addition to improved equipment performance and reduced costs, TPM also affects employee attitudes. Comments received in our survey[10] included "Teamwork between maintenance and operators has improved," and "There is greater employee satisfaction." Increased job satisfaction through improved skills and more interaction among employees is noted by Edgar Schein[11] and others who have researched the subject of employee involvement.

KEEPING THE CUSTOMER HAPPY

Customer satisfaction was also mentioned by a number of the companies as one of the rewards of TPM. Providing a service to a customer is as important as making the initial sale. When the glass globe of a recently purchased camping lantern was broken, the purchaser found that the replacement part was not available at any store within a 100-mile radius. A sales associate from the store where the customer purchased the lantern replaced the globe with one from a new item so the customer would have it in time for an upcoming camping trip. The customer later referred a relative to the store for other purchases.

Satisfied customers do a great deal for the continuous well-being of a company, while disgruntled ones do considerably more harm. Technical Assistance Research Programs, Inc., found that unhappy customers share their discontent with nine to ten people. Since it costs five times more to get a new customer than to keep an existing one, it is critical to develop customer satisfaction and loyalty.[12]

Internal Customers

The same philosophy is true for internal customers, as well as external ones. It is remarkable to observe some workers' lack of concern for or interest in their peers' opinions of the quality and quantity of their work for their internal customers' satisfaction. In every industry, each employee serves at least one customer — usually the next person in the process. Internal customers are often fellow employees, and their satisfaction or disgruntled attitude will spread to others with whom they work or come in contact. If equipment fails, the details of the problem are quickly embellished and widely known, for the customer has been disappointed. The focus of TPM on equipment reliability forestalls these problems. Properly functioning equipment enables the worker to accomplish assigned tasks, generating satisfaction in a job well done.

BENEFITING OURSELVES

Some companies mentioned increased problem solving and reduced paperwork as additional benefits of TPM. As workers gain experience, their problem-solving abilities grow, further reducing the costs associated with troubleshooting. As machine operators take over routine maintenance tasks and equipment performs with greater efficiency, the number of work orders from malfunctioning or failed equipment decreases. When malfunctions and breakdowns diminish, so do associated paperwork and documentation.

In searching further, we found others also noting the benefits of TPM. John Roe, of IRD Mechanalysis, believes predictive maintenance shows a return on investment in three to six months, figuring conservatively.[13] According to an article in *Plant Engineering*, computerized maintenance management alone can generate a 5 to 15 percent reduction in the overall maintenance budget in addition to reductions in other areas, such as scrap generation.[14] Authors Harold Amrine, J.A. Ritchey, and C.L. Moody state that 75 percent of maintenance problems can be prevented by machine operators trained to detect them at an early stage.[15] Nissan attributed a savings of $400,000 to TPM in 1986. This was accomplished by an 80 percent reduction in equipment breakdowns and a 20 percent reduction in labor-hours, including a 12.5 percent reduction in maintenance personnel, while the reject rate fell from 0.6 to 0.1 percent. Machine operators devote only about 3 percent of their time to TPM.[16] The list could go on.

Because TPM encompasses all aspects of maintenance management, the benefits of its various components combine to make the comprehensive strategy extremely powerful. Proper management can reduce life-cycle cost of both equipment and facilities. Maintenance labor-hours, inventory, downtime, repairs, scrap rates, and energy consumption are among the areas in which costs can be reduced and that can provide the greatest return on investment.

No one can predict how much the savings will be for each industry, particularly without hard data. Data must be collected for comparison purposes as the change takes place. Unfortunately, most companies have no idea how much their maintenance costs. These expenses are buried or ignored because they are not tied directly to product cost. Start-up costs will be highest for those who have ignored the importance of maintenance. They have the most to correct.

Poorly trained workers cannot function in a fully operational TPM strategy. Poorly maintained equipment *must* be brought up to established standards before the benefits of TPM can be seen. The longer these details are ignored, the longer it will be before any gains are realized. An antiques collector knows that those pieces that have *always* been cared for and require no restoration have the greatest value. Some pieces, however, are worth the cost of extensive restoration. Those who are willing to invest in the effort reap enormous benefits. Many of our industries need extensive restoration, but they are operating under a leadership too shortsighted to see the possibilities that exist beneath the surface.

If we can find this much information about the benefits of TPM, we can only wonder how much greater the gains really are. Although we have barely scratched the surface, we are convinced that the TPM strategy is the key to economic survival for all businesses. It applies to both production equipment and facilities systems equipment. The more machine intensive the industry, the greater the impact.

Satisfied customers at all levels are essential to a profitable organization. Even service businesses like motels, restaurants, construction firms, airlines, and retail stores cannot satisfy their

customers if their heating or air conditioning systems fail in severe weather as a result of poor predictive or preventive maintenance. TPM is the foundation for that satisfaction, from the
environment in which it operates to the efficiency and reliability
of the machinery or equipment being used.

PART II

Getting Started

7

Understanding Change: The People Problem

The most difficult aspect of implementing TPM is to get everyone in the organization to recognize the need for change and to commit themselves to it. Though people may casually acknowledge the fact that no growth can occur apart from change, it becomes a different matter when that change involves them personally. Change is frightening, as well as unnerving, uncomfortable, and threatening. But it is also necessary and inevitable. We tend to make too much of it, not recognizing that change is a fact of life.

PERSONALITIES AND CHANGE

Change will happen whether we like it or not. If we do not accept this, we will be controlled by change instead of controlling the process ourselves. Feelings of helplessness and hopelessness generated by attempts to avoid change are devastating, while the willingness to embrace positive change can be rejuvenating. By focusing on its positive aspects, change, like exercise, can be good for us even if we don't like it.

The change process becomes further complicated because each of us differs in our reaction to it. While some of us get excited and embrace the challenge immediately, others react more cautiously. Thus, orchestrating a change such as TPM is like trying to get a band to march in time with the music when each musician is playing at a different tempo. In the United States we are proud of our cultural values of individualism and competitive spirit. Sometimes we focus so much on individuality that we become immersed in what pleases us and ignore the viewpoints of others. We tend to forget that our strength can also be a weakness. With each of our rights, however, there is a corresponding responsibility. The right to work carries the responsibility to do that work well. The right to a safe, pleasant work environment requires that we, individually and collectively, maintain that environment. The right to make decisions about our futures demands that we exercise the responsibility for actively participating in the change process.

Change is not always easy; for some, it is never easy. We can, however, make it less difficult if we accept it as an integral part of life. We also need to recognize that we cannot always choose the change in which we will be asked to participate. We may choose where we live and work, who we marry or play golf with, or how we use our free time. Some changes that require our participation, however, are orchestrated by others. In such instances, our response is determined by our reaction to authority and to other external controls. Employees who resent being told what to do will balk at a change initiated at a higher level. Many will resist any change suggested by another. Those who are uncomfortable with the group or team process will find it difficult to participate in group or team decisions.

The status quo is comfortable for most of us. We are familiar with the demands placed on us and our ability to meet them. This was brought home recently when we spoke with a group of junior high school students. Given the possibility of being the "best," they decided they preferred to be in the middle. Being the worst was unappealing, but being the best, whether in school or at work, would cause them to stand out from others and make them feel uncomfortable. They felt they lived in the best country in the world already and saw no relationship between the future of their country and their desire to perform in comfortable mediocrity. Fortunately, this is not the attitude of all our youth, and hopefully this group will also develop a more mature viewpoint in the future.

Unfortunately, our greatest dilemma is not that a group of young people should feel most comfortable with the status quo. At their age, the need to belong and be like others is at its peak. The real tragedy is that many adults also hold similar immature views. The only way to overcome this kind of inertia is to disturb their complacency and change their view of the future.

Recognizing the Need for Change

The first step in initiating change is creating dissatisfaction with things as they are. In the case of TPM and other world-class strategies, this dissatisfaction will vary, depending on the group within the organization. For the CEO and board of directors, it may come from the loss of competitive edge or loss of profits. For the worker, it may be generated by smaller or fewer pay raises or the loss of jobs. When everyone is satisfied, no one sees the need for change. Only when disaster is imminent and life-styles are threatened can change be quickly initiated and massive gains made.

If it becomes known publicly that a company is on the verge of failure or of filing for reorganization to avoid bankruptcy, a new unity and desire for change can suddenly emerge to not only salvage the company but actually make it stronger. Such was the case with Harley-Davidson. Others have been less fortunate and have had to close their doors. Managers blame the workers for not accepting change, and the workers blame it all on management — a lose-lose situation. Some, like the G.E.

Microwave Division, concluded that it was cheaper to contract with overseas competitors than to change. Ultimately, this too resulted in closed doors. The lesson to learn is that in order to survive, every person in the company must meet the competition head on, accepting the challenges and making the changes necessary to overcome all obstacles.

Apart from a threat to its survival, an organization must determine the extent of its danger and the amount of time available before it also is threatened by competition. Lead time during which a company has no competition for a new product is now only a few months. Missing the target for getting the product to market can mean losing the market completely. One well-known company had no competition 15 years ago. Little attention was paid when its first competitor entered the market. It now has five major competitors, one of which is located in the same city! Whether the company is currently in mortal danger does not really matter. What does matter is that change is essential to counteract the pressures it now faces.

If a company is not in imminent danger, the initial phases of the change process should be carefully orchestrated. Those who understand the need for change must communicate it to the unaware and the disinterested. They must impart a sense of urgency to the others. The need must have a high profile, especially if the advocates for change are few. *TPM is a high-profile need*. It is possible for one or two people to recognize that need, share their concern with others, and effect widespread change over time. Change is never instantaneous, and in the case of TPM, it will require a minimum of three to five years, possibly as many as ten.

Presenting the need for change means more than saying, "This is why we should do it." People must be made to realize that their assumptions are wrong and enough tension and anxiety must be generated to motivate a change in behavior. They also must feel safe in order to give up those old responses and adopt new ones. Each individual needs time to decide whether he or she can comfortably live with the new attitudes and behaviors and whether the changes will be reinforced by others. Peer support is essential to sustain any change in individual or corporate behavior. It is important to provide consistent advocates and champions for the change who can serve as mentors to others and furnish information from a variety of sources to validate the need for change.

THE EMOTIONAL ASPECT OF CHANGE

The tension and anxiety caused by change is a factor that must be recognized whenever a company adopts a new organizational strategy. Consideration of emotional and psychological factors is especially important in the development of a TPM strategy because it involves such a radical departure from traditional ways of thinking and doing business. Indeed, the problems involved in establishing TPM are primarily people problems associated with the change process.

Machine operators fear more work as they are confronted with the idea of performing machine maintenance tasks. Maintenance personnel worry about losing their jobs if they relinquish tasks to machine operators. Workers do not want to retrain or to learn new work patterns for a variety of reasons. Some do not read well or find learning more difficult than they care to admit. Others are concerned that retraining requires part of this education to be done on their own time or at their own expense.

These anxieties need to be refocused so that workers realize that without both individual and corporate change, there soon may be *no* jobs. If a company cannot operate profitably, it cannot operate at all and will cease to exist!

CHANGE AND EDUCATION

Even though they are currently employed, workers in every field of endeavor and vocation must recognize the ongoing need to retrain and upgrade skills in order to maintain their employability. Who would want to use an accountant familiar only with tax laws of 1965, a physician who did not keep pace with the changes in modern medicine, or a secretary who considers manual typewriter skills adequate for a busy insurance office?

The demands of our technical information society are expanding so rapidly that industrial and professional leaders must rethink their positions on education. Eighty percent of the skills of those now working in technical areas will be obsolete in three to five years. If we continue to value leisure and family time, at least part of the educational burden must be borne by the business community.

U.S. manufacturers spend less on training than their overseas counterparts. This puts a greater portion of continuing education in after-work hours, which can become a burden for those who want to be involved with family and community. Since stress and burnout are directly related to a lack of balance between work and leisure, it makes good economic sense to provide a work environment that promotes balance.

The flip side of this argument is that workers in the United States are less apt to devote leisure time to further education. Our society does not recognize study as something to applaud. Our literature, movies, television, etc. often treat studious individuals as "nerds" or people to mock or pity. The dilemma is that employer and employee attitudes are so closely intertwined that it is difficult for either group to begin the change.

Education should be a shared responsibility, as it is vital to the success of the organization and the individual. Workers should take advantage of opportunities for improvement provided by their employer and should also look for opportunities to improve through their own initiative.

People who refuse to acknowledge the importance of continuing education are a detriment to their own well-being as well as that of their families, employers, and community. We know many employees who refuse to take skill-improvement courses because they already have jobs and see no need to learn more to keep them. In an environment primarily dependent on physical ability, such an attitude is understandable. However, our world demands a different level of involvement. Today's global economy requires employers and employees alike to invest in education and training.

THE CHALLENGE OF TRAINING THE EMPLOYEES OF THE FUTURE

In conversing with a small group of teenage students whose academic skills were below grade level for various reasons, it quickly became evident that their attitude of doing only what is necessary to get by is the result of a feeling of hopelessness. They see little opportunity for themselves as adults because of their weak academic record. They want to believe that being the best that they can will be enough, but they are not sure. Once they believe that, with effort, they *can* learn, they will accomplish more than anyone dreams.

Many adults are similar to this group of young students. They do not want to admit to the difficulties they face with academic tasks. Instead, they take the attitude that, having completed school, they need no further education. These barriers can be broken by planning educational opportunities that allow them to learn and overcome deficiencies while maintaining their dignity and sense of worth. Once the industries for which they work realize that they have the potential for doing more and give them the opportunity to do so, the costs of training programs will be offset.

The United States needs a highly trained work force, but does not have one. The vast majority of workers have little opportunity for formal education or for informal training after they enter the work force. Even companies with excellent education and training programs take the attitude that learning new skills is fine as long as it does not interfere with production.

Researchers have found that seminars and training opportunities are usually reserved for the managerial and engineering ranks. While these people need to keep abreast of changes in their fields, those directly connected with production also need to improve their skills and understanding of economics and competition if the company is to survive. Workers who understand the pressures of global economics are willing to work with management to implement the changes necessary for survival.

Some managers would insist on transferring a clerk, forklift driver, or custodian to a production machine maintenance mechanic position if the employee's previous position has been eliminated. While the policy of redeploying displaced employees is admirable, thought must be given to the difference in technical skills required, whether the transferred employee even has mechanical abilities, or how long real training might take. The overriding concern, however, is that the individual continue to work.

This may be very noble. It is also very foolish. It is like asking the company cook or corporate counsel to run the computer system. These people may be outstanding workers in their areas of expertise, but this does not mean they are qualified for other areas. The employee's job is now in real jeopardy because of lack of adequate skills for the new position.

The people who make these redeployment decisions are often the first to demand that their personal dentist or physician be trained in the latest skills; no one wants a trainee performing their brain surgery. Such practices can weaken the company that engages in them, the individuals who are inappropriately employed, and society as a whole. These do not add value and cannot be tolerated in a company seeking world-class status.

Workers need to feel valued for their expertise in positions to which they are assigned. Inappropriate deployment of human resources sends the message that the positions involved are unimportant or that anyone can do it. As a result, these workers may gain a false sense of their own importance, failing to recognize their own limitations, or they may recognize their limitations and develop feelings of inferiority and incapability.

On top of this, children whose parents are victims of such redeployment are exposed to a false model of the world of work. If the parent is placed inappropriately, the children may decide that there is little relationship between education and work and therefore little need for effort in the classroom.

In addition, another individual who has become qualified in a variety of skills may wonder if the time and energy expended in obtaining that education was worth it if workers are transferred because management's priority is to retain its work force at the expense of obtaining people genuinely qualified for the positions in which they are placed.

It is as essential for management to put a high priority on training as it is for the employees to have good basic work skills and a willingness to learn. To delay training or support it only as long as the company does not have to pay the employee for added knowledge and skills is to continue the unconscionable deskilling and belittling of our workers and our children.

This is especially important for total productive maintenance because many people fail to recognize the importance of maintenance. Management sees it as a non–value-added component and gives it little consideration particularly in training budgets. Because we expect our machines to run, we give them no thought until they quit, or we find we don't know how to operate them. Providing training time, funds, and opportunities for TPM is one of the best ways to let employees know TPM is vital to the organization.

TPM Training Helps Stop Job Abuse

In addition to workers who do not want to enhance their skills, there are those who try to keep fellow employees from doing so as well. They ridicule company training programs and those who take the classes. They intimidate new employees or temporary workers, telling them to work more slowly because they don't want more expected of them.

One young man who went to work for a manufacturing company after graduation from high school was given a brief orientation on operating his machine — and a much more detailed lesson on how to precipitate a breakdown, along with a code for his turn to do so. After being physically threatened, he joined the breakdown conspiracy so everyone on the line could have a 30-minute break while maintenance personnel went through complicated trouble-shooting, corrective action, and restart procedures.

A functional TPM strategy does not permit such abuse because machine operators have responsibility for the routine maintenance, inspection, minor adjustment, and operation of equipment. When a major problem occurs that requires a maintenance technician, the operator provides input and assists as much as possible in the repairs. The attitudinal changes accompanying the advent of TPM preclude the previously described problems as it becomes fashionable to improve rather than destroy production results.

MEANINGFUL CHANGE

The attitude of the future is that training is essential to production. An educated work force understands when the need for change is presented, thereby shortening the time needed for initiating and instituting change. An educated work force has the learning skills necessary to absorb and apply new information. With a current base of knowledge, it takes less time to learn specific applications since it is easier to transfer previous learning than to begin learning from a base of little or no prior knowledge.

As management sees the value of a highly trained work force, it is more likely to maintain those skill levels. We must realize that skills are subject to the same constraints as the product market itself. New technologies can make new skills obsolete within months after training is complete. Practice and continuing education are essential.

8

Three Stages of Change: Initiation, Implementation, and Institutionalization

INITIATION: COMMUNICATING THE IMPORTANCE OF CHANGE

Much of what happens during the initiation stage in the change process involves communicating and raising awareness of the need for TPM; this must be done at every level. If executive personnel do not understand the importance of TPM, they will undermine it at every turn, out of ignorance if nothing else. How can you support something you don't understand?

The operations manager who is concerned only with the production numbers and ignores the need for quality will ultimately destroy the company. The line supervisor who repeatedly delays training to increase production or meet schedules will find that those who put training first will ultimately achieve the most. The worker who considers training a waste of time and wants little or no responsibility may soon have his or her wish granted — and lose the paycheck as well.

In this initiation stage, people need to be made aware of two facts: that there is always a place in an organization for those who are willing to grow with it and that there is no place in a world-class company for an individual who clings to the ways of the past or does no more than the minimum required by a job description or contract.

When the culture of a company is firmly entrenched, it is far more difficult to orchestrate change than it is in an emerging organization. There will be active resistance to change, greater demand for extra pay to participate in training programs, complaints about changes in work assignments, and many forms of passive resistance. "We've always done it that way." "It won't work." "Management just has another stupid gimmick." "The workers are opposed. . . . " "How much more will I get paid?" "That's not my job." "We've got to meet the production schedule first. Maybe sometime after the first of the year." "We've just let all our temps go and can't release anyone for training right now." "Profits are down — we can't afford to." "It's just an excuse to get rid of maintenance people." "We really don't have time right now." The excuses go on and on.

Advocates and champions of TPM succeed by taking on one argument at a time — as it occurs. Whether these advocates come from the work force or are members of a designated TPM staff makes little difference at this point. They must somehow get the attention of the entire work force. The more vocal TPM supporters become, the sooner the doubters will be able to share the vision. Once one group of workers realizes TPM's importance and benefits, it can carry the TPM torch — provided it has upper-management support. *TPM must be supported from the top while it is driven from the bottom.*

IMPLEMENTATION: GETTING STARTED

Some companies will spend thousands of dollars forming elaborate committees to study those aspects of TPM they wish to implement first. Others will take a more spontaneous approach with little start-up investment. Tennessee Eastman was among the first to recognize the need for TPM; the company spent a half-million dollars to develop and implement their

TPM strategies.[1] Other companies with less generous resources have proved that it can be done, though more painfully, with minimal funding for start-up costs. One company we visited is using an advocate-champions networking model in which training is being developed and conducted in-house and presented to the workers by their peers. This is definitely the "slow boat" model and not recommended because implementation is so much slower than when assisted by external experts. Longer implementation time reduces the gains that could have been realized and increases the risk of being overtaken by competition. Some middle approach, using appropriate outside help, is best.

Regardless of the model used, those spearheading the effort must have a thorough understanding of the change process. Failure to recognize that people react differently to change, that organizational growth, like physical development, is uneven, and that regression does not mean certain death, will frustrate and discourage those who have made a heavy personal investment. Not understanding the change process will defeat a movement for change faster than anything else.

No matter how the change process is approached, once management and workers have accepted the logic of TPM, the move to implementation becomes a natural outgrowth of the need, which is now recognized as a necessity for *survival*. The attitudinal change may be subtle at first, but it will be strong enough to allow for action. It will often be expressed in the development of new maintenance procedures and training machine operators in the care of their equipment. It may take the form of installation of a computerized maintenance management system (CMMS) or the organization of a preventive maintenance program. For some, it might simply be improved housekeeping.

Recognizing Success

Successful implementation depends more on thoroughness than on scope. Success breeds success. Once workers see positive results from their efforts, they will be encouraged to participate further. Once management sees changes in attitudes and reductions in costs, they will become stronger advocates of TPM.

Success is part of the implementation stage, and so is disenchantment and discouragement. Therefore, those who participate in TPM implementation need support in every way possible. Recognition should be given for participation in training, for the generation of ideas, for involvement in statistical process control classes, for modification of existing processes or creation of new ones, and for historical data collection. Rewards should also be considered in areas of leadership, stamina, fortitude, and for anything else that will hasten the development and implementation of a TPM strategy.

Recognition need not be costly or sophisticated to be appreciated, but it must be *sincere*. It may be a handshake and a "thank-you" from the CEO or other member of the executive staff. It may be in the form of a certificate of accomplishment, recognition in the company newsletter or newspaper, a picture and suitable comments on company bulletin boards, a gift certificate at a local store or restaurant, something for a person's hobby, or a cash award or bonus check. Give pocket calculators — perfect for statistical process control and analysis.

It may not be popular to say so, but companies need to share economic gains with the employees who make those gains possible. Those organizations that implement massive change in a time of crisis may have asked employees to take cuts in pay or benefits to help the company survive. When the crisis is past, those people should be the first to receive a financial payback for their efforts.

Stockholders may wait anxiously for increases in profits. They need to wait a little longer, for investing a dollar in the company is not quite the same as investing yourself. The greediness of stockholders is part of the reason some companies are in trouble. It has been unpopular in recent years to reinvest excess corporate profits back into the company, but rewarding employees enhances loyalty and involvement so that, in the end, the company becomes even stronger and stockholder earnings grow even more solid.

The Pace of Implementation

The more quickly an organization can move from initiation to implementation, the better it is for morale. Realistic time lines for implementation need to be established and adhered to as much as possible so that workers can see the need still exists and is being addressed. It is common to move through an initial project with enthusiasm from the pilot group and then to lose momentum as the project nears completion. Because it is impossible to sustain 100 percent efficiency from people, TPM project teams can be changed to give more individuals a chance to experience involvement with the development of the strategy. Building in a "rest period" to give employees time to assimilate the impact of the change can also be helpful.

Burnout is most possible and dangerous when advocates and champions are few. Thus, it is essential to expand the group and to plan strategy meetings, bull sessions, and so on, for encouragement and reinforcement. When one individual is feeling "down" and that momentum is slipping, another can point out where gains and successes have taken place.

Just as equipment has a life cycle, people also have change or growth cycles. Recognizing these cycles and working with them rather than against them is important. A friend who manages a large segment of his organization has said that each of us is capable of giving different things at different times in our lives, and we can best meet our corporate goals by accepting these differences. By being sensitive to them, we will actually speed the change process.

When people are allowed to move through change at their own pace, they are less threatened by it. Those presenting the change must recognize that sometimes ideas must be proposed at least three times — first, to refuse it as totally impossible; second, to hear what is being presented and give it consideration;

and finally, to decide to give the idea a try. A TPM leader cannot get frustrated while waiting for acceptance, nor upset when an individual who is slow in coming to terms with the change forgets that he or she was initially against it. He or she recognizes that individuals respond differently to leadership styles and try to provide the kind of leadership that will promote the most growth for each individual and work unit.

Ups and Downs

Understanding the change cycle makes it possible to establish realistic time lines and to anticipate problems that will occur as TPM is developed within an organization. Though advocates and champions may be few at first and that group may grow slowly in the initial stages of the change, something suddenly happens in the networking process. It is like reaching critical mass. An explosion of effort takes place. Champions appear in areas where there were none. Implementation moves forward in spite of those who are still opposed to any form of change. Then, for some reason, the bubble bursts.

Implementation seems to be happening too slowly. The champions see setbacks and opposition. They become frustrated because others are not cooperating or changing fast enough. Because the group has grown larger, the burnout problem will be larger. However, there will also be more supporters to help one another over the rough spots, to support the strategy, and to continue developing champions until the next critical mass is reached.

As implementation of one aspect of TPM takes hold, the need for its other elements will become apparent. If the initial need presented is "TPM," in all its facets, there will be no problem in addressing another segment of the strategy. It will be just another strand in the change cycle. If, however, the need was presented in terms of a single element of TPM, such as preventive maintenance, employees will think management has shifted focus and abandoned the first element when it comes time to institute another element of the strategy. When the entire need is presented on the front side, people will realize that doing everything at once is impossible. They will be more willing to break the task into manageable segments, and they will see the new focus as another part of the same strategy.

INSTITUTIONALIZATION: THIS IS THE WAY IT'S DONE

Implementation is a time for testing procedures to see how well the new methods work. At this stage, flaws are detected and adjustments are made. Once this is done, the change has become institutionalized and it is now part of the organization's way of doing business. It becomes a standard or benchmark against which performance is judged and it is so routine that new employees don't know that things were ever different.

Institutionalization may come quickly or may take several years, depending on the complexity of the change. We have found that institutionalization takes time for most companies. Even those at the forefront of TPM do not admit to having reached a final stage. The changes that were initially targeted have become institutionalized, but other needs are now being addressed. They attacked the most critical problems first and moved on to tackle other things when the initial items were at or near institutionalization.

This does not mean that TPM is institutionalized when those initial problems are corrected — only that one aspect of TPM is achieved. Because TPM encompasses so much, it takes time to fully implement all five components of the strategy. It involves far more than sporadic efforts for improvement. The acquisition of a new CMMS program, statistical analysis procedures and equipment, and the like are elements of a TPM strategy just as arms and legs are parts of the body. Each must be exercised to develop strength. Just as young people can improve their strength more quickly than their elders, young organizations can achieve institutionalization more quickly than older companies whose work force is already set in their individual behavior patterns.

When entrenchment is a hindrance to progress, those who refuse to change should be allowed to move to an area in the company where they will be less involved with change. If this is not possible, they need to seek employment with a company where attitudes are more similar to theirs. The MIT Commission on Industrial Productivity found that the organizational patterns and attitudes that are at the root of productivity problems are difficult to change, even when the need to do so is recognized.[2] Therefore, it is essential to remove those who would block progressive change in an important undertaking such as the implementation of TPM. This includes employees at all levels who refuse to participate in the change process.

If the change is important, people must be willing to make that change happen. We cannot live with our heads in the sand. Yesterday's products have already been sold and become obsolete. The present is here only for today. Tomorrow is ever before us. We must prepare for its challenges or we will be unable to survive.

Without change, there is no growth. When we stop growing, we begin to die.

9

Maintenance Prevention: "No Problem!"

DÉJÀ VU

This car is a real gem — fully loaded, even has a CD player! Fantastic acceleration! . . . You say you like to do your own maintenance? Nobody bothers with that anymore. It's just too darn complicated. No, not even oil changes. The filter is above the front axle so you'd need a hoist to get to it from underneath. Besides, the car sits so low you can't crawl under it. Spark plugs? There are six; four of them aren't too hard to get at, but the other two . . . without a special wrench and a hoist, forget it. You still say you want to do your own maintenance? Well, good luck! You want to look around some more? You'll never find a sweeter deal than this. Why worry about maintenance on a new car?

Maintenance? No need to worry. The maintenance and repair manual explains all you'll ever need to know about this machine. True, it's not very detailed, but who cares? It's just less junk to have lying

around, and who likes to read such boring stuff anyway? You'll never remember it. No, you don't need to
have your technician specially trained to work on this
machine. It'll never break down. Just run it 'til it dies.
You'll like the way it's designed. It's the latest in technology; does everything but start itself. No one else
has it yet or knows anything about it. It will put you
on the cutting edge of technology.

Such scenarios with salespeople are all too common. It's
easy to say maintenance is "no problem," because, in reality, no
one cares until it becomes a necessity — when something
breaks. Suddenly, a catastrophe has occurred and the maintenance technician is supposed to pull magic out of a tool box and
fix it. *Maintenance prevention* is that aspect of TPM that addresses
the need to design equipment for maintainability so that it can
operate for an extended period of time before it requires attention. In many instances, preventive maintenance is all but impossible because maintenance prevention was ignored during
the design stage.

LEARNING FROM HINDSIGHT

Consider the effort and planning that goes into building a
house. We know several people who have decided to dabble in
the construction business by being the general contractor for
their new homes. One couple thought it would be easy to find a
set of commercial blueprints for a house that fit their ideas. They
planned to purchase the blueprints and build accordingly. That
was their first big surprise! Not one of the hundreds of plans
they examined fit their requirements. It was similar to looking
for a piece of standardized production equipment already designed for specific production needs, although no one in the
world had any idea what the production needs might be.

After careful consideration, they decided to draw plans
themselves to fit their needs. They discussed ideas and asked

for input from several people to ensure nothing vital was over-looked. They made scale drawings of the floor plan and even of the furniture to assure adequate room sizes. Then they "walked through" the house to check that traffic patterns were smooth.

How many engineers take such an approach to equipment they decide to design? A thorough study of requirements may be time consuming. In this house-building venture, the initial planning took much longer than anticipated. Using existing plans would have saved time, but all of the known flaws and unwanted features would have been built into the house. So it is with production equipment. If engineers who design machines or purchase premanufactured machines from another company do not do their homework properly, all the flaws that could be avoided are built in. If planning and teamwork are inadequate in the design stages, the machine will be a source of frustration and high maintenance expense throughout its life.

Design According to Need

Experience on the plant floor tells us that few equipment design engineers pay attention to real production requirements, just as most architects fail to consider all the cook's needs when designing a kitchen. They may put in lovely cabinets, but there are too few of them and they are in the wrong places. Appliances may use the latest design and technology, but there may be less than two feet of continuous counter space. We were in a friend's home recently where the stove was at least 15 feet from the sink, giving the cook a daily aerobic workout.

Like architects, design engineers must pay attention to myriad details. What is the purpose of the machine? What is the simplest way for it to function? How much space will it require? Does it need air or water, and how about the type of electrical power? Is the area adequately designed for the machine? What about ventilation, heating, cooling, and lighting? What are the needs of the operators? Does it make too much noise? . . . and on and on.

Some questions can be answered only by those who have used or worked on similar equipment. These people may also supply answers to questions that no one else would even think to ask. Good designers must go beyond considering such elements as repetitive motion, lifting, standing or sitting by the operator, and safety. They should not work in isolation but rather constantly seek input from those who use and maintain the equipment and from those who determine its performance limits.

The Cost of Poor Planning

The design engineer who positioned 23 air lines directly in front of an electrical access panel gave no thought to how a technician would gain access to the panel when troubleshooting an electrical problem. The machine was installed on the plant floor before the flaw was noticed. Redesign, like remodeling, is always more expensive than the initial construction. Added to modification or redesign costs is the cost of dismantling the original mistake and working around things that cannot be changed. Had maintenance prevention been in place where this engineer worked, the problem might have been detected early in the design by a member of the team. Correction would have been simpler and less costly, and the engineer would have suffered far less embarrassment.

FALSE ECONOMY

While asking questions is a major part of a design or manufacturing engineer's job, listening is also vital. A school district asked for input on preliminary design for a new school several years ago. Teachers and others explained carefully what they thought should be changed, only to be told their suggestions could not be used. Since the building's completion, several major changes have been made in response to needs presented by teachers — many of which had been presented and rejected in the initial design phases. When a major remodeling project was undertaken, more improvements were made, but some major problems could not be corrected because of cost or basic structural design. Maintenance prevention would have saved many taxpayer dollars and provided the teachers the satisfaction of seeing some of their original suggestions incorporated into the initial design.

A Window of Opportunity

Maintenance prevention is an area of great opportunity for U.S. manufacturing industries. Companies that have been in existence for a long time are being forced to replace aging equipment. New companies have a unique opportunity to do things right the first time. Through state-of-the-art design technologies and teamwork, as well as allocation of money necessary to acquire the most applicable machine, modification and maintenance costs will be minimized.

Medical expenses will be greatly reduced when equipment is also ergonomically designed with operator health and well-being in mind. Fewer hours will be lost to minor ailments; there will be fewer accidents, and speed will be more easily maintained. Insurance premiums may be reduced due to lower accident rates and fewer medical claims. Most important to the customers, fewer accidents and injuries mean that projected delivery times will be more reliable.

To accurately reflect costs, we need to remember that inflation costs must also be factored into future repairs, downtime, and lost sales. Comparing the real cost of higher-priced, maintenance-free machines with lower-priced, less-reliable machines that cause more production bottlenecks and demand more maintenance may prove that the more costly machine is actually the best buy. Only after considering all factors is it possible to make a realistic judgment about real maintenance costs.

If industry is to take advantage of opportunities provided by maintenance prevention, a new attitude toward the acquisition of equipment must be adopted. Super machines that do everything may make engineers feel they have created something wonderful, when in fact they have spawned monsters. The "KISS" principle (keep it simple, stupid!) is always the best. Simple design and operation of the machine simplifies maintenance. Simple parts and simple repairs equal reduced maintenance costs.

Practicality and Realism in Design

This simplicity principle cannot be carried too far. The more it is possible to standardize parts for different machines, the better it will be for everyone. The cost of repair parts to support these machines drops due to lower spare parts inventories. When motors, bearings, springs, duraslides, tooling, microprocessors, and associated electronic components are standardized, training time to learn installation, operation, and maintenance is reduced. Operators and technicians are exposed to fewer types of high-technology equipment, but they have a more thorough knowledge of that equipment. They will also be more capable of synthesizing their knowledge for application in a variety of situations.

As engineers ask questions and listen carefully, they can help reduce unnecessary equipment maintenance costs. They can, for example, design leak-proof gearboxes by using bearings and seals of the latest design. They can investigate machinery they plan to purchase from a vendor, checking for ease of maintenance and the service life of components in the complete machine or in the subassemblies purchased to build a machine in-house. A machine that breaks down is a poorly designed machine. Even if the breakdowns are for short periods, they can result in a bottleneck and loss of revenue.

Besides bringing in prebuilt machines (with minimal information regarding installation and operation) for setup by maintenance technicians, engineers are often guilty of assembling a variety of "widgets" from many different companies into one complicated machine. They may know the purpose of each component, but they give little thought about how the machine will operate, its service life, how easily it can be repaired or replaced, or how long it may be available in the marketplace. The life-cycle cost of such a machine can be computed only by considering each part separately and in relation to each other.

Engineers designing equipment should be so thoroughly familiar with all aspects of the machinery that they can explain each feature to the machine operators and maintenance technicians who will ultimately be responsible for keeping the machine running at peak efficiency. If engineers with 16 to 20 years of education and higher degrees do not understand the operation of the equipment, how can they expect those with far less training and experience to do so? Problems like these should be addressed even when machinery is purchased from a vendor specializing in large, complex, or technologically advanced equipment.

One of the greatest problems in equipment design is that applications change quickly. Massive production runs are no longer feasible because of the high costs of raw goods and finished inventory. An engineer, like the designer of maternity fashions, knows that needs can change daily. Allowance must be made for these changes to make equipment cost effective. Product appearance may not change, but the material it is made of may have to change because of availability, environmental concerns, or cost. Changing user requirements also create shorter life cycles for products. No one can afford to be stuck with thousands of dollars of obsolete product.

In this era of constant change, engineers must keep in mind a number of considerations. Will the machine operate under changing conditions? What kind of modifications are required to accommodate these changes? Are these modifications easy to make, how long would they take, and how much do they cost? Do changes in material or machine adaptations increase production time, have an adverse or positive effect on quality, or result in increased or decreased scrap rates? Finally, how long does a production line have to shut down to make these changes, and how do they affect such factors as tolerances and appearance?

TOTAL EMPLOYEE INVOLVEMENT FOR ENGINEERS

Applying the Golden Rule is in order and could solve lots of problems. Engineers should design machines as if they had to operate and maintain them. "If my hand won't fit here, neither will someone else's. If I find this motion tiring, so will someone else. If I can't figure this out quickly, how can I expect a machine operator or maintenance technician to do so? If I can't get this part to work, others will have the same problem. If I can't understand these instructions, neither can anyone else." Written instructions must also be clear and drawings easy to understand. They should be updated to incorporate a variety of details previously ignored.

Such thinking involves a revolution in the way people interact. Engineers most frequently talk to other engineers. Machine operators discuss their frustrations with other operators. Maintenance technicians are too busy trying to repair all the broken machines to care about scheduling needs. People must be willing to work together and talk to each other instead of protecting individual interests or territories. Turf wars and empire building must end.

Everyone who has any involvement with production, scheduling, operation, maintenance, purchasing, and design of production machines must work as a team to determine the best way to get the job done. This involvement must be ongoing and include all aspects of each project. Then, when a new machine is installed on the plant floor, the engineer is not solely responsible if it doesn't work. When the walls of mistrust and lack of communication are torn down, the engineer can get assistance in the problem-solving stage because everyone has a vested interest in getting the equipment to operate properly.

Although maintenance prevention applies only to new equipment, it is nevertheless essential to smooth production flow throughout the life of the equipment. A mistake made here is a lifelong mistake, and anyone who chooses to bypass maintenance prevention opts for a multitude of unforeseen problems.

Once equipment is installed on the shop floor, there is no further opportunity for reaping the benefits of maintenance prevention. If given proper initial consideration, the dividends of reduced maintenance costs continue during the life of the machine. If maintenance prevention is ignored, however, the mistake can never be fully rectified. The consequences are costly and inevitable.

THE ROLE OF AN EQUIPMENT MANUFACTURER IN MAINTENANCE PREVENTION

In our search for companies that are striving for world-class status, we found some unique applications of systematic maintenance strategies. Some of these companies have begun designing new equipment in-house because of their specialized needs. Others prefer to purchase new machinery from an equipment manufacturer that can meet their needs. Custom equipment manufacturers, by the nature of their business, are in an ideal position to do maintenance prevention. Because they produce one-of-a-kind equipment for someone else's use, they are not subject to the constraints, such as mass-production delivery deadlines, that affect most manufacturing industries.

One refreshing young company, TechniStar Corp., of Longmont, Colorado, embraces all components of TPM as a matter of good manufacturing practice. TechniStar does not use labels such as TEI, TQM, or TPM; implementation of these world-class strategies is tailored to the company's internal needs.

As a fast-growing producer of integrated flexible robotic automation systems, TechniStar has developed a global customer base over a short time. By targeting customers within related markets, it has been able to expand its expertise in providing equipment that can perform in special environments such as airline-meal packaging. The company designs for automation because research predicts that by 1997 there will not be a labor force willing to do repetitive service jobs such as meal packaging. TechniStar's customers pay for reliability and the TechniStar reputation; technology is the result.

Commitment to quality is a driving force in the organization, beginning with the hiring of employees. Though innovation and creativity are essential in a young growth industry, many companies overlook the need for people willing to do routine or unglamorous tasks as well as the more creative ones. For example, instruction manual preparation may not be an engineer's favorite task, but it is high on the list of tasks that must be done well. Careful hiring practices provide the opportunity for moving ahead of older companies struggling with an entrenched work force.

Because TechniStar builds extremely high-tech equipment for other industries, it must furnish detailed instructions, including carefully written technical manuals, and provide skills training to machine operators and maintenance people for maintenance of their products. The company also maintains high standards of quality maintenance for its own equipment. Recognizing the importance of elevating maintenance to the status it needs, TechniStar has developed a corporate hierarchy that unites maintenance and service under the direction of Jerry Swisher, senior vice president of operations and services. According to Swisher and Senior Vice President Miles Snyder, the service group reports to upper management to reinforce the importance of quality service and customer satisfaction.

Maintenance prevention requires a commitment to good design. In product development, consideration is given to the universe of errors that could occur. Since customers equate a product with the manufacturer, products must meet or exceed customer expectations. TechniStar is one of few companies that becomes directly involved in helping set customer expectations. The company wants its equipment used to its fullest capabilities. Poor design means lost product sales, so the emphasis is on designing equipment that will function without need for modification after it's installed and operating. Thus, maintenance prevention is reduced to its simplest forms: foresight, early planning, common sense, and good manufacturing practices.

Initially at TechniStar, predictive maintenance was a nonissue in its usual forms of vibration analysis, oil analysis, thermography, etc., because flexible robotics relies heavily on microprocessors and advanced electronics. Predictive maintenance is, however, tied to preventive maintenance guidelines established for each unit. Determining appropriate preventive maintenance schedules is impossible without considering predictive maintenance. Guesswork puts preventive maintenance on a par with the lottery; if you're lucky, you get it right.

TechniStar's involvement in corrective maintenance is limited to adaptations necessary to accommodate the new equipment at the customer's installation site. Preventive maintenance and autonomous maintenance are the responsibility of the customer. The primary concern for TechniStar as the equipment builder is that the customer's TPM strategy is compatible with and enhances the performance of the purchased equipment.

TechniStar, like many equipment manufacturers, offers a service contract on its products, but with a unique twist. Recognizing the importance of satisfied customers, the company includes training costs related to equipment maintenance and operation in the basic price of the machine. Few customers turn down training for which they have already paid. After-sale service is also given careful attention. TechniStar solicits feedback from its customers whenever possible, not only when problems arise.

Companies building their own equipment would do well to apply similar strategies. Whether equipment is purchased or built in-house, those who design equipment are providing a service and a product to a customer, even when the customer is internal. By recognizing the importance of maintenance prevention as an element of TPM, equipment designers do much to support the other components of the TPM strategy.

10

Predictive Maintenance:
A Stitch in Time

Maintenance prevention alone does not solve all maintenance problems. The ideal situation links maintenance prevention with the other elements of TPM. Only this scenario can achieve maximum benefits.

When equipment replacement is not an option, using the other TPM components is even more essential. Though the other components may not generate the savings that maintenance prevention does, these approaches can make the difference between staying in business or going bankrupt. They determine how long and how efficiently equipment operates.

A CRYSTAL BALL THAT WORKS

If a problem cannot be prevented, the next best thing is to know when it will occur. Since no car runs indefinitely on one tank of gas, we can avoid running out of fuel by predicting when that event might occur. This can be done by filling the tank, driving until the tank is empty, calculating the miles per gallon, and then carefully monitoring the miles driven in the future.

Thankfully, such a strategy is not necessary. A handy predictive device — the fuel gauge — has been developed to constantly monitor and report the fuel level; it is also more reliable because it monitors consumption under existing conditions. A driver crossing Kansas once found that his gas mileage was reduced by more than half when he traveled into the wind during a severe windstorm. The gauge indicated that the car's gas consumption had increased, so he refueled more often. By maintaining adequate fuel levels, he avoided costs of road service and lost time as well as the dangers of being stranded in a storm.

Predictive maintenance is the crystal ball of manufacturing. Good predictive maintenance allows us to determine how long equipment will run before it goes out of tolerance, needs lubricating, tuning, adjusting, overhauling, or replacing.

RECOGNIZING DISCREPANCIES

Predictive maintenance is a science dependent on many people along with sophisticated and simple instrumentation. Like maintenance prevention, it requires input from a variety of sources. Quality can exist only when every person is aware of what constitutes a threat to the integrity of the process.

Thus, data collection is essential at all times. If we don't know what normal is, how will we recognize the abnormal? Like an expert who learns to recognize counterfeit bills by carefully studying the genuine article, we can only recognize what is wrong by knowing what is right. While some discrepancies can be identified visually or by auditory signals, such as changes in loudness, pitch, or timbre, other problems can be detected only with sensitive instruments.

Statistical process analysis cannot be overemphasized; it provides the evidence that machines are operating properly and processes are working smoothly, from the receipt of raw materials to the shipment of finished goods. Machine performance must be measured to determine its accuracy. This can require costly instruments, especially when checking internal conditions.

Majoring in Minors

Minor problems, if ignored, become major problems. Since physically detecting many problems before a certain level of degradation has occurred is impossible, statistical process control is the only means of detecting errors early. Vibration analysis is much more accurate than the human ear or sense of touch. Though diligent record keeping and monitoring may seem costly, they will ultimately save money, improve morale among workers as they understand the importance of equipment performance, and delight customers in search of quality.

Besides verifying quality production, statistical process control can also verify quality service. Service measurements are simpler to collect than product quality measurements, often requiring only classification and counting. How many units are returned during a given period? What are the complaints? How many service calls are made? What parts of the country have the most complaints? Are the complaints about product quality, delivery, customer service, manuals, or something else? Employees can collect service data and store it on a computer. Of course, if nothing more is done with the information, the time spent collecting it is wasted. To be of value, the data must be used.

Employee Involvement in Data Collection

Enthusiastic employees who understand the importance of statistical process analysis are essential to the success of every organization. Apathetic employees are more destructive than those who openly refuse to participate — at least you know what they aren't doing. Those who don't care may or may not record information, or they may choose to "guesstimate" rather than take an actual reading. Such contamination of data renders it worthless.

If any part of an organization is satisfied with being less than the best, it will have a negative effect on the rest of the company. The attitude that minor problems can be overlooked or that only production numbers matter can spell doom for everyone. It can't be said too often: making a bad product is worse than making nothing! If employees are not committed to enthusiastically doing their best, they need to look elsewhere for work. They do not belong in your organization because they are undermining your credibility with your customers.

The entire organization must be committed to the same goals at all times. If production is working to improve quality and reduce waste while marketing is making unreasonable promises to get a sale, or accounting is adding layers of management just as others are asked to remove them, morale will quickly plummet. Improved quality and reduced waste must be the standard for everyone.

WHERE TO FIND THE SAVINGS

Recognizing when equipment will fail is important since breakdown maintenance is much more expensive than scheduled maintenance. But predictive maintenance goes beyond that initial prediction by providing the information for determining the most appropriate course of action. Through awareness of a developing problem, changes in planned maintenance activities can prevent unscheduled downtime. Gearbox repairs are a common savings area in predictive maintenance.

Cost savings due to predictive maintenance comes from a number of areas. Tabulated dollars saved are only a part of the total savings. As machines operate more efficiently, fewer repairs make it possible to reduce spare parts inventory. Wages of operators lost to downtime and of maintenance technicians for extensive repairs are reduced. The savings from reduced energy costs, increased equipment efficiency, reduced waste or scrap, and increased customer satisfaction are more difficult to measure but no less real.

GETTING THE MOST OUT OF PREDICTIVE MAINTENANCE

As with other aspects of TPM, starting big in predictive maintenance can be self-defeating. It is better to target a single machine or line and be thorough in what you do. *Collect data, data, and more data.* Record everything. How many times does the operator make a specific adjustment? How long does it take? What is the interval between adjustments? Which parts are replaced? How long has it been since the last replacement? Only when you have accurate data will you be able to determine what needs attention. Over time, it becomes obvious that some data is irrelevant and can be dropped from the collection process. Initially, knowing what is important is difficult to determine. Collecting unnecessary data is better than ignoring something that could be important.

The techniques used for predictive maintenance differ from industry to industry and from one operation to another within an organization. Savings are greatest where equipment costs are greatest. A company that depends on large equipment that performs multiple sequential operations will gain more from thorough predictive maintenance than a business that uses many small tooling machines. When continuous operation is critical, predictive maintenance is essential.

Methods for measuring machine condition are as varied as the equipment used in manufacturing. There are, however, a few major categories, each of which deserves specific investigation according to organizational needs. Our purpose here is not to provide that detailed information but to suggest areas for further research. Vibration analysis, thermography, eddy current testing, sound analysis, and spectrum analysis are several methods for detecting problems before they are noticeable.

Vibration analysis is used primarily to determine wear on shafts, bearings, and other elements of rotating machinery. It is the leader in predictive maintenance because it can reveal a wider range of faults than any other procedure. Methods for measuring vibrations also vary. Monitoring machine condition can be done at a number of points and can prove useful even with new equipment, as one company discovered when the bearing supplier changed the tolerance slightly without changing the part number. This is not uncommon; however, it does indicate the need for continuous monitoring as well as the importance of working closely with certified ship-to-stock vendors.

The selection of appropriate equipment and process parameters for measurement determines the success of vibration analysis. Spectrum, waveform, or orbit analysis may be required; this can be determined only by evaluating current and future measurement needs. Static data collection systems work well and are relatively inexpensive for many applications. Dynamic data collection systems may be more expensive but are necessary for more sophisticated measurements. Hand-held systems are less expensive than computer-based systems, although the data is less dependable. If you are just beginning a predictive maintenance strategy, you may be able to achieve impressive results with rather primitive instrumentation; however, as success rates increase, so does your need for more sophisticated measurement capability.

Lubrication analysis is a means of determining lubricant as well as machine condition. Samples may be sent to a commercial laboratory for analysis if the company does not maintain a laboratory capable of this type of testing.

As with vibration analysis, there are several types of lubrication analysis. Particle counting, direct-reading ferrography, and analytical ferrography can be supported by spectro-analysis, viscosity, and infrared analysis to determine levels of oxidation, metal contamination, water, and so on. Wear-particle analysis helps determine causes of wear through size, shape, and type of material found in the lubricant, making it possible to bypass teardowns and zero in on the part needing repair or overhaul.

Eddy current testing involves setting up magnetic fields by alternating electrical currents within the tubes of air conditioners, condensers, heat exchangers, and the like, in order to locate defects in the tubes. An oscilloscope records the signals that help identify the type and location of damage, so repair costs can be minimized.

Temperature measurements are more widely used in daily predictive maintenance. Equipment, like the human body, has a normal working temperature. Changes in temperature indicate a problem and may provide clues regarding what might be wrong. Thermal analysis can be used to prevent overloads that cause equipment shutdowns, pinpoint appropriate maintenance intervals, identify the location and type of weaknesses, and determine when replacement is necessary.

Stress analysis, boroscopic inspection, and frequency measurements along with many other equipment-specific tests can also be used for predictive maintenance.

TRAINING: COST VERSUS SAVINGS

As measurement capability needs increase, so do training requirements. Maintenance personnel must learn how to use the equipment and analyze the data obtained. Vibration analysis, especially, will increase maintenance costs, in terms of both time and training, because the work must be done in-house. It cannot be sent out to a laboratory and charged to a different account. New technology requires new training and new skills. These do not come cheap, but the costs are far less than the money spent to replace equipment that has worn out prematurely or lost revenues due to downtime caused by malfunctions. Sometimes the result of finding a single problem is sufficient to pay for test equipment and/or training costs.

Whatever predictive maintenance techniques are used, they need to be linked to a computerized maintenance management system for data collection and control. At the very least, a company should institute programs to train everyone involved in recording or interpreting data, so they can perform those tasks competently and confidently. Predictive maintenance is only as good as those who use it.

11

Corrective Maintenance:
If It Ain't Broke, Fix It Anyway

Corrective maintenance, like maintenance prevention and predictive maintenance, relies heavily on engineering expertise — in this instance, to modify equipment effectively. While there are many similarities between predictive and corrective maintenance, the difference lies in motivation. Predictive maintenance is aimed at determining how long equipment will function, while corrective maintenance seeks ways to improve function, whether or not breakdown is imminent. Corrective maintenance is designed to reveal and eliminate malfunctions and their causes, resulting in improved machine performance and reliability.

Why Modify?

Modification of machinery is routine in many situations. Modifying equipment before or as a part of the installation is often necessary when adapting it for a specific application. Modifications may be dictated by space requirements, energy demands, ventilation, relationships to other production equipment, changes in material, or design changes in the product, as well as by safety concerns and adjustments in quality standards. Adherence to federal regulations is another factor that must be considered.

Getting Better

The most important aspect of corrective maintenance, however, is continuous improvement. A team dedicated to quality engineering can improve performance through a variety of corrections. Adjustments in the speed of conveyor belts may even out work flow, whereas repositioning a machine might make it easier to change molds. One company reduced its installed cost of insulation by thousands of dollars when it switched to a different material that possessed higher thermal efficiency.

In another company, the motor in the product was a significant portion of product cost. A corrective maintenance team, consisting of an engineer, an electronics specialist, and a maintenance technician, began studying the assembly process to determine why there were huge amounts of rework, scrap, and downtime. As they talked with workers and observed and analyzed problem areas, it became evident that the arc welding machines were not welding rivets properly. Welds would be partial or missing. Doing a 100 percent inspection was necessary to sort good product from bad. The welding machines frequently misfired because they were not suited to the task.

The old welders were replaced with new state-of-the-art machines. Sensors and an industrial microprocessor were added. Other processes were smoothed out through retooling or redesign.

This instance blended corrective maintenance with maintenance prevention. Because of their age, rebuilding the old welders was not a viable solution to the problem. Corrective maintenance for the product line demanded new welding technology. Maintenance prevention became a factor in selecting the new welders.

The results surpassed everyone's expectations. Production is now consistent and continuous. Machine reliability and quality have increased while rework and waste have decreased. Scrap was reduced by 97 percent and rework by 92 percent, generating a savings of over $15,000 per year due to reductions in material, labor, and maintenance costs. A 2 percent reduction in costs is equal to a 7.5 percent increase in sales.

As soon as this project was completed, the team focused on another problem. A microprocessor was shutting down one machine, and subsequently seven other machines linked to it, effectively stopping two production lines. Once the microprocessor was upgraded, machine rejects have been reduced from 60 percent to 1 percent, uptime has increased 50 to 70 percent, and machine assembly error has been eliminated.

In addition to the documented statistical improvements, workers have noted that the line runs smoother, more product is produced per hour, and quality is easier to control. The team has moved on to other projects, and success stories continue.

HIDDEN MAINTENANCE COSTS

Only one member of the above-mentioned team is dedicated to corrective maintenance on a full-time basis. Others join in according to specific needs and in addition to other assignments. Together they eliminate repair work that would become their responsibility, saving several times the salary of an engineer over a year's time. Dollars generated by increased quality, worker satisfaction, and customer goodwill are additional bonuses for the company.

Unfortunately, unless it is dictated by federal regulation or a loss of production, corrective maintenance is often overlooked. Although it may cost extra to hire someone to identify problem areas and make the necessary corrections — repairs are never cheap — corrective repair is much less costly than downtime repair.

While corrective maintenance has an impact on both the visible and the hidden costs of maintenance, the hidden costs are affected most. Likewise, any gains that are realized often go unrecognized. The "if it ain't broke, don't fix it" mentality degrades product quality, hinders production, and causes equipment and facilities to deteriorate at an accelerated rate.

INGENUITY AND HARD WORK

Corrective maintenance is often a test of ingenuity. Making changes in existing equipment is far more difficult than changing a blueprint. Skilled engineers find ways to make workable modifications that most of us either ignore, don't see a need for, or don't understand. They work with technicians and operators to make equipment operation smoother, safer, and more efficient.

Corrections may require major modifications, or they may be as simple as adjusting the speed of a conveyor belt, changing the type of printing ink used, or adjusting weight tolerances to accommodate a change in material. If slowing the speed at which a product moves through the production process reduces or eliminates equipment jams so that workers can focus on a steady flow of quality goods, it actually becomes easier to produce more with less waste.

Improving the System

Some of the most spectacular corrective maintenance has been done by the U.S. military and NASA. Repairs and changes to Skylab, the Hubble telescope, and the space shuttle are examples of corrective maintenance that have required a wide range of expertise. Corrective maintenance has extended the life and usefulness of U.S. aircraft, including the B-52; it has also enabled the military to turn "dumb" bombs into "smart" ones.

Corrective maintenance is the essence of recalls of automobiles, appliances, and tools. When a malfunction, safety problem, or part failure is discovered, corrections are made to increase the product's safety, improve its performance, or lengthen its life. As consumers, we prefer to purchase defect-free products, but we appreciate the security of knowing that corrective maintenance comes with the purchase.

Corrective maintenance is equally important for the producer. Whether the new part is a component of the product or of the machine that produces it, the result is improved product quality and reduced costs.

AVOIDING CORRECTIONS

Corrective maintenance is similar to the treatment of a child born with a turned-in foot due to its position in the womb. If the problem is recognized and treated immediately, it may be corrected within a few weeks. If treatment is delayed until the child is walking, however, it may take many months, or even years, to alleviate the problem. This longer treatment is more costly, in addition to being more painful.

Though maintenance prevention and predictive maintenance may seem more ideal than corrective maintenance, they cannot solve all problems. A mother who guards her health during pregnancy cannot control the position of the unborn child; corrective care may be necessary. Similarly, the need for some corrections to a machine may not be apparent until equipment is on-line and actually producing. It is important to recognize the need for a correction and to make it in a timely manner.

Corrective maintenance is as integral to TPM as the heart, lungs, and other vital organs are to the human body. If one part does not function properly, life itself is endangered.

12

Preventive Maintenance: Do or Die

Preventive maintenance might actually be called the fore-runner of TPM. Mechanics learned early that regular oil changes extended engine life, just as any housekeeper knows that sweeping and cleaning carpets makes them look better and last longer than those that do not receive such care. It is like drinking enough water, getting enough sleep, eating balanced meals, and exercising to prevent illness.

TRADITION!

For industry, preventive maintenance minimizes equipment deterioration by scheduling maintenance to minimize wear and breakdowns. It is the traditional approach to maintenance, which recognizes that oil and lube is a cheap way to keep equipment from breaking. Changing the air filter, the worn fan belt, or the tires prevents a breakdown at an inconvenient or dangerous time and place.

A World-Class Act

Obviously, preventive maintenance is necessary. In the study we performed comparing Colorado companies with organizations recognized as world class, we investigated how preventive maintenance is used in relation to other components of TPM. We found that most companies aspiring to world-class status have improved their preventive maintenance by adding computerized maintenance management systems. We also found that production personnel usually release equipment for preventive maintenance only under duress. All the companies that reported using some form of TPM cited this as the number-one problem. Issues about employees' attitudes accounted for half the problems mentioned.

Although equipment is the focus, attitudes impact implementation. The individual who sees no need for preventive maintenance will not bother to change a furnace filter, defrost a freezer, add attic insulation, repaint a house, mow the lawn, or wash the dog. Fleas, weeds, rotten siding, or heat loss may result, but the correlation between these consequences and the failure to take appropriate preventive action may go unnoticed.

Preventive maintenance is, above all, a commonsense method for maintaining smooth performance of the equipment or facility. It can be accomplished only when people care about what they do, take pride in their work, assume responsibility for quality, and seek continual improvement. Preventive maintenance takes place when there is teamwork and a willingness to defer short-term gains in favor of long-term objectives. The time saved by failing to fill the gas tank is quickly lost when you run out of gas in the middle of nowhere. The cost of calling a locksmith when a key is lost is much greater than the price of a spare key. The cost of lubricating a machine is far less than buying a new one. An attitude of "fix it so it won't break" on the part of employees may be an important factor in containing expenses and remaining profitable.

KEEPING A COMPETITIVE EDGE

Preventive maintenance is the heart of TPM and the core of every maintenance strategy. Without the continual care of equipment, early gains can suddenly be lost.

Equipment cannot be maintained if it is never allowed to stop running. Production managers are right to be concerned about meeting production requirements. Too often, however, their concern is misguided. Getting out the numbers is not enough; sometimes it is the worst thing to do. Meeting the day's schedule for 150,000 parts is disastrous if 149,000 are bad! True, it would have cost money to force a machine shutdown, but making junk costs even more.

If scheduled downtime costs are one-third of breakdown costs, consider how much more expensive it is to run a bad product, consuming labor and raw materials for nothing. In a country where labor costs are high, rework is an unbearable expense that can be avoided only if equipment continually operates at peak performance.

Data Collection — Again!

As in other aspects of TPM, record keeping is an important part of preventive maintenance. Since companies use desktop computers to track parts, schedule routine maintenance, document malfunctions, and so on, technicians need to maintain basic software skills and to accurately log data, either directly on the computer or for data entry at another time.

Accuracy is absolutely essential. Some technicians make cursory inspections and sign off on scheduled procedures without actually performing the required maintenance because it appears that nothing needed to be done. When the purpose is prevention, the work must be done *before* a problem arises. Failure to recognize the importance of preventive maintenance, either by those in production or by those in maintenance, cancels out TPM.

GETTING IT TOGETHER

Having part of a strategy is like having part of a car. You won't get far if the engine is missing. Preventive maintenance and computerization are necessary components; but, like an engine and two wheels, they don't make an automobile. Even together, they do not equal TPM.

13

Autonomous Maintenance: Abolishing the Fiefdoms

The phrase "last but not least" definitely applies to autonomous maintenance; it is the most elemental component of TPM — the backbone of the strategy. Autonomous maintenance gives machine operators the freedom to make decisions about machine performance and adjustments based on those decisions as well as the opportunity to increase their knowledge and understanding of the equipment they operate.

Autonomous maintenance demands that workers move out of the comfort zone of the status quo. The struggle for change takes place within the individual as well as the organization. Personal change requires the acceptance of new responsibilities and challenges in the face of peer resistance. Organizational changes threaten ingrained networks and hierarchies. The rewards and risks at this level are enormous.

CHANGING TIMES

In the early days of manufacturing, assembly line workers did many rote tasks by hand. As machinery became available that was capable of performing those tasks faster and more accurately, workers on assembly lines became machine operators. They were required to push buttons, operate levers, and do myriad mindless tasks until the equipment broke down. The work was as mindless as it was before mechanization and much less personal. Paychecks often became far more important than the satisfaction of a job well-done.

As more assembly and production operations are turned over to robots, workers who were once subject to the pain and boredom of repetitive-motion tasks are being freed to take on more interesting and challenging responsibilities. However, this new freedom may not always be welcome, as repetitive jobs seldom guarantee pride of workmanship or any sense of ownership in the final product.

If this is the case, it may be necessary to show employees reasons to help justify making the change. Increased awareness of medical problems such as carpal tunnel syndrome and tendinitis may help workers realize that the old jobs were not only boring but also painful or disabling. In addition, the astronomical cost of treating these problems is a drain on profits and the ability to provide increased pay.

A REASON TO DO WELL

Autonomous maintenance does away with lackadaisical attitudes once machine operators get past the "It's not my job" syndrome. Machine operators are given responsibility for the equipment and for production quality; they are the ones who check production, rather than someone at the end of the process; and they now have a greater level of accountability for their work. Machine operators also have more authority and freedom to make decisions. Instead of calling a technician to oil a bearing, they can do it themselves, once they receive sufficient training.

Moreover, machine operators can tell more about the condition of a piece of equipment than anyone else in the company. The regular driver of a car is familiar with its noises, vibrations, and temperature. Any change will be recognized earlier by that person than by an occasional fill-in or casual observer. Even a mechanic may have trouble recognizing visual, auditory, or tactile signs of trouble until the problem escalates.

Robots have taken over much routine assembly work since they can operate at a steady pace indefinitely and are more cost-effective for rote tasks. On many modern assembly lines, workers monitor the robotics output and perform more complex tasks than in the past. As their jobs become more complex, their need for training increases. Training makes the difference between job satisfaction and frustration.

PREPARING TO DO WELL

Training is the key to the success of autonomous maintenance as well as the other TPM components. Training cannot be a hit-and-miss affair. Some companies provide training as a fill-in activity when equipment fails. Others train new hires for one or two days. Companies may assign training as an additional task for someone who has another job to avoid the costs of maintaining a training staff. This is not training.

Training is recognizing that changing technology demands changing skills. Training is realizing that many of those in today's work force must cope with technology that did not exist when they were in school. Most schools have had computers for little more than a decade and are only now getting enough terminals to use them in areas other than programming or business classes. How can we expect employees to understand or effectively use what they have never been exposed to?

Asking machine operators or maintenance technicians to log or retrieve data requires training on two levels. They must first understand the purpose of the data and then learn how to use the software. This type of training takes more than an hour or even a day; it must be ongoing and must be arranged to allow practice between sessions, which should be spaced closely

enough together to maintain interest but far enough apart to
allow for learning at the application level. Training must be designed to accommodate learning styles and to ensure maximum
retention of the material covered.

To keep up with technology, retraining is needed every
five to seven years. The auto mechanic who had to comprehend
5,000 pages of information 20 years ago must now contend
with 465,000 pages of pertinent data.[1] Corporate training must
take this explosion of information into account when developing programs.

Training must be job specific as well as ongoing. Our
school systems are not the best vehicles for imparting job-spe-
cific skills to students — most specific job skills are obsolete
within five years. Instead, schools should prepare students
with a deep foundation of general knowledge. Companies
should expect to provide training specific to their organization's needs, while expecting employees to bring with them
and maintain a general base of knowledge.

Training is the life-blood that stimulates and revitalizes. It
is the alarm clock that reminds us of the importance of keeping
our skills up to date. It should not be left to outsiders, nor
should it be the added-on responsibility of someone who has
another primary job and little expertise as a trainer. Trainers
need dual skills and should be recognized for their unique talents. They must know what they are teaching and they must be
skilled teachers. We have all suffered through presentations by
people who knew their subjects but did not know how to present the information. Workers will consider poorly taught classes
a waste of time. If training is not important enough to do well, it
is not really important to the organization.

When Workers Don't Care

Not everyone places the same value on education and
training. Some employees are nearing retirement and will be
gone before training can be completed. Understandably, they

may have little desire to participate in what they may never use. A transfer to another area may be most appropriate for them.

Some workers are complacent. Their attitude is "don't bother me," "let someone else do it," or "forget night school." They are more interested in their weekend activities than in their work. Having graduated from high school, they believe they have all the education they need; more training would simply waste their time. Though it may take time, such deadweights must be removed for their own long-term good as well as that of the organization. Until they realize that the old approaches are no longer adequate, their attitude will undermine morale and productivity.

The Ready and Willing

Other employees are eager to participate in new technologies but lack training. They should be given opportunities to learn before their enthusiasm wanes. They should be encouraged to expand their capabilities as much as possible — and be rewarded for their efforts. Workers who know the importance of continual training and enjoy learning can become discouraged by negative peer pressure. They need support and encouragement to hold on to their ideals.

COPING WITH CHANGE

Companies that have had the greatest success in improving production are those, like Harley-Davidson, which have been in the greatest difficulty. Change is never easy, and autonomous maintenance is a big change. It is a radical move from noninvolvement to total involvement, from isolation to collaboration, and from dependence to independence. While autonomous maintenance provides workers with independence and greater control over the equipment they operate, it is based on shared knowledge and expertise.

A greater level of cooperation is required of everyone. The production manager must have confidence in the operator's decision to shut down his or her machine. The operator must be able to articulate the problem, and the technician must be able to recognize and solve the problem.

In autonomous maintenance, there are differences in function but not in importance. The success of one is the success of all, and the failure of one is the failure of all. It has long been said that two heads are better than one. Autonomous maintenance capitalizes on that truism.

PART III

Conclusions

14

Progress:
Who Is Doing TPM?

Perhaps the greatest way the United States differs from other nations is in its view of traditions. As a people, we tend to value the new more than the old. Because we are a relatively young nation, we lack ties that demand we do things as they have always been done. We have lived in a changing world as our borders expanded, our government grew, the industrial revolution brought continuing technological changes, and education was made available to everyone.

WHO HAS THE VISION?

It is easy to get enthusiastic about a new idea. But sustaining that momentum until the idea has matured and become an institutionalized change is difficult. Often we give up or switch our efforts to another cause before the first has a chance to prove its worth. We have seen this in recent years as we have moved from an industrial-based to an information-based society. We have embraced the Deming philosophy, quality circles, teamwork, employee involvement, quality control, site-based management, networking, kanbans, focused factories, computerized maintenance management, and a host of other concepts and buzzwords related to improving quality and reducing waste in our various enterprises.

Many of these strategies come under the umbrella of the basic principles encompassed in world-class manufacturing. Companies that embrace these strategies have a keen awareness of the effects of global competition on their businesses. We have found that larger organizations pay the most attention to world-class strategies. Companies in heavily industrialized areas are also more aware of WCM than those in areas with diversified economies.

WHAT ARE THEY DOING?

Just-in-time is the most popular component of world-class manufacturing, with total quality management running a close second. Those who pursue continuous improvement most vigorously find they cannot maintain quality and a smooth production flow without employee involvement and a comprehensive maintenance strategy. Total productive maintenance nevertheless lags behind the other strategies in most companies.

As with other world-class strategies, smaller companies are less apt to see the need for TPM. Many tend to degrade maintenance rather than to elevate it to a level that recognizes its underlying importance. TPM is not flashy; its customers are internal rather than external, so there is no visible connection to profits. TPM is seen as overhead, a cost center rather than a profit center. In addition, mechanical work is often dirty, and some view anything dirty as demeaning; however, it took a lot of dirty mechanical expertise to put a human on the moon — and to win a war in Iraq. Our best and brightest do not always wear white shirts and three-piece suits. If they did, none of us would survive.

Companies' increasing awareness of the importance of maintenance strategies in relation to production is both encouraging and frightening: encouraging because the number of companies making significant gains in this area is rapidly increasing and frightening to think of what will happen to those that have not yet realized the need to do something or who are dabbling with a halfhearted commitment to change.

WHO NEEDS TO MAKE A BUCK?

In a world of fragile economic balances, companies must pay attention to their markets and search constantly for ways to improve quality while reducing costs. Instead of looking for one way to save a million dollars, managers must now look for a million ways to save one dollar. *TPM is probably the last of the million-dollar savings strategies.* It also provides opportunities for myriad small savings. Companies incapable of large savings strategies due to such factors as their size frequently overlook smaller opportunities. They believe that because of their size or the nature of their business, TPM does not apply to them.

We contend that TPM applies to everyone. Every business has some maintenance expense, even if most of this cost is in the facility. The strategies that apply to production equipment operation translate into facilities equipment as well, such as heating and air conditioning. Employees involved in continuous improvement can reduce janitorial costs in the way they approach their tasks. Some relatively new buildings look much older than they should because of improper care. At the same time, there are older buildings that appear to be new after 20 or 30 years of use.

FACILITIES TPM: THE UNTAPPED RESOURCE

By attending to all the TPM strategies with regard to the facility itself, companies can tap another source of significant cost reduction, especially for those with lighter production requirements. Unfortunately, TPM for facilities is ignored by all but the most astute.

Companies that have begun pursuing ISO 9000 certification are among the leaders in the adoption of TPM. Because they have a visionary approach to their business, they look for opportunities to make gains in all areas. We have observed that the companies unfamiliar with the standardization and quality demands of ISO 9000 are the same companies that have overlooked world-class manufacturing approaches. These companies fail to realize that by falling out of step with the rest of the world, we hurt only ourselves.

WHO IS DOING TPM?

Companies that hope to stay in business for more than a decade are discovering the advantages of incorporating TPM into their strategies. They are the ones who thrive on change and look for new ways to meet existing challenges. They are the companies with leaders who have the will to succeed and the courage and vision to try something different. They are the ones with management teams willing to take risks and tolerate mistakes, the ones that want to be better than the best — and that are willing to make their organizations the best by encouraging everyone within those organizations to realize their fullest potential. These companies are the ones who have a vision of the world, not as it is, but as it can be.

15

Case Studies: TPM In Action

In our research into what companies are doing with TPM, we found that data is locked up and generally inaccessible to outside organizations. Companies do not want to share numbers or percentages that might give their competitors an edge, nor do they want their flaws exploited. These are legitimate concerns in today's global environment, where economic survival is more difficult than it was a few decades ago.

Some companies that initially succeeded with JIT are now losing their edge. Although we have no hard data, sources suggest that these companies pay little or no attention to TPM. They give lip service to the strategy but have been unable to sustain a consistent, ongoing commitment to fully implement TPM, primarily because senior management fails to see the need.

There are two types of companies that usually commit to some form of TPM: companies that have stood at the brink of disaster and survived and new companies looking for a slice of the pie. Few older companies have been able to avoid the pinch completely. Good and lean times come to us all for one reason or another. Some companies look at difficulty and see a great opportunity, while others simply tighten their belts and try to muddle through. New companies have the luxury of deciding how to become world class without the traumas of aging facilities and machines, outdated technologies, or entrenched attitudes in the work force.

HARLEY-DAVIDSON MOTOR COMPANY, MILWAUKEE, WISCONSIN

Harley-Davidson is one of the best-known companies to recover from disaster. Certainly few organizations have been closer to death and yet made such a spectacular recovery. The company is proof that corporate culture can change quickly when the need is great enough.

The lessons Harley-Davidson learned and shared with the world are vital to the success of every organization:

- People *must* be trained for the work they do.
- Change is painful. It takes time.
- Improvement isn't enough. It must be continuous.
- Short-term management undermines any company.
- If you wait for a competitor to take the important risk first, you are doomed.
- Those who cannot accept change must not be allowed to hinder the process. They need to find an environment where they can be comfortable.
- Do things right the first time.
- Senior management must support change if it is to occur.

Although Harley-Davidson learned these lessons well, TPM was overlooked in the early days of its rebirth. Focusing on continuous improvement eventually led them into TPM. They saw the need for TPM to support just-in-time and total quality management.

Like many organizations, Harley-Davidson began by implementing preventive maintenance and a computerized maintenance management system. Machine operators received training and the company now has a world-class lubrication program in place. After five years of refining the skills of maintenance personnel and machine operators, the company is turning its attention to predictive maintenance. Corrective maintenance has already become a new area of focus for a team currently performing preventive maintenance.

TPM has created less machine downtime, more machine operator involvement, and improved attitudes on the shop floor. At first, operators didn't consider TPM activities part of their job. Maintenance personnel worried about job security, and production management did not consider maintenance activities as important as production. Experience and time are helping eliminate these concerns.

Autonomous maintenance has been achieved in lubrication and is spreading to other areas. Extensive training is conducted on the plant floor at each machine to enhance learning. Maintenance calls for housekeeping and lubrication-related activities have been significantly reduced, resulting in less unscheduled downtime, which is an ongoing concern.

Facilities manager Wayne Vaughn, PE, believes that a well-run TPM program will eliminate 80 to 90 percent of regular maintenance calls and that within three years the TPM team can help reduce unplanned downtime by a factor of 10. Downtime will never be eliminated, but it should be planned to improve machine performance or quality.

We believe that Wayne Vaughn and the Harley-Davidson team will achieve the goals they have established because CEO Richard Teerlink, board chairman Vaughn Beals, and other members of the senior management team support their people and the continuous improvement strategies of world-class manufacturing.

ALLEN-BRADLEY CO., INC., INDUSTRIAL CONTROL GROUP, MILWAUKEE, WISCONSIN

Allen-Bradley Co., Inc., a Rockwell International company, has weathered ups and downs of the economy for nearly 90 years. The company's Industrial Control Group (ICG) has moved successfully from the techniques of early assembly line production to a highly automated technology in the production of its industrial and automation control products, changing both products and the processes to meet customer needs.

Before TPM, Allen-Bradley faced the constraints of aging equipment and entrenched attitudes among the work force. Today, Allen-Bradley has achieved world-class status by blending automation and just-in-time concepts. The company has maintained an enviable position by continuing to improve and expand its world-class strategies.

Some people say that large, long-established, unionized companies cannot develop TPM strategies because of the size of the organization, union resistance, and aging equipment. Allen-Bradley has proved them wrong. Cooperation among unions, management, and workers is essential to success in such a large organization — and it does not happen overnight.

In the initial stage of TPM at the Industrial Control Group, inventories and floor space requirements were reduced. Higher-quality service resulted in fewer callbacks and heightened response to customer needs. Despite such noticeable results, it has taken three years to bring about an attitudinal change in the corporate culture throughout the site.

The problem of worker attitudes is common in many organizations. During the period of rapid growth in the 1950s and 1960s, people who had good technical skills were promoted to job classifications tailored for their qualifications. Though excellent workers and competent as technicians, they lacked adequate training for positions such as engineers or troubleshooters. Some did not want to become involved in change because they were nearing retirement; others were resistant to the need for further education.

These problems have been addressed and are being overcome through some innovative training approaches. Training budgets, which were already substantial, have increased by 60 percent in the last two years. Training for maintenance personnel focuses on electrical and mechanical areas; for equipment operators it centers on the care of production machines. Having developed a TPM strategy that encompasses all five components, R.L. Quigley, director of facilities and plant engineering, states that the facility is now focusing on three areas: "Training, training, and training."

To enhance training efforts within the company, ICG has developed a close working relationship with the local schools to improve vocational programs. Management believes it makes sense to use existing sources through mutually beneficial industry-education partnerships. Schools are not up on advancing technology, in part because industry does not vocalize its needs. Allen-Bradley now provides equipment and technically skilled people to help train students so that they have the equivalent of a technical school diploma or associate's degree on completion of the program.

The company addresses the problems of aging equipment through predictive, preventive, and corrective maintenance as long as these strategies are practical. When the upkeep on a machine is no longer economical, the equipment is replaced. Maintenance prevention is then given careful attention in designing or selecting new equipment, with technicians involved at each step of the design process.

By using world-class strategies, Allen-Bradley has reduced production times for some product lines from a matter of weeks to as little as a day. To achieve and sustain such results, equipment must function at optimal levels. Recognizing the importance of understanding financial performance measurements, such as return on investment and return on assets in relation to profitability, Quigley worked with the finance area to restructure budgets to make them understandable to maintenance as well as accounting personnel. Maintenance personnel also receive intensive training in general accounting practices so that they grasp the financial impact of wasting resources. Cost information is translated into pie charts so that everyone can see the maintenance labor costs and the reasons for them. This information, along with historical data, is invaluable when justifying requests for capital equipment or the dollars to put into the standard expense budget.

Though support for TPM from unions, workers, management, and accounting is necessary, TPM cannot be achieved without initial support from senior management. According to Quigley, "If your vice-president of operations isn't tuned in to TPM, it will be difficult to contain future maintenance costs. It [TPM] requires management's full support for the program up front." Quigley is fortunate — his vice president of operations is clearly tuned in.

EATON CORPORATION, HYDRAULICS DIVISION, EDEN PRAIRIE, MINNESOTA

Eaton Corporation's Hydraulics Division sets an example for others faced with resistance to change. People are empowered to change, but there are no demands on those who choose not to embrace TPM. Like Allen-Bradley, the focus at Eaton is on training. Employees take a three-day course in how products are made, what the products are for, and how they work. By understanding the product's function and design, employees develop a sense of ownership and pride in their work. Education also helps employees (many of whom have been with the company 17 to 20 years) understand the need for continuous improvement.

Since TPM was adopted at Eaton, outside contract repairs have declined, machine downtime for repair has decreased, and control of operating costs has improved. TPM has also provided an opportunity to make environment-friendly changes, such as eliminating the use of chemicals, solvents, and their accompanying air emissions.

Although the company is involved with all phases of TPM and senior management recognizes that TPM is a major part of any world-class strategy, there is still work to be done. Eaton believes in self-evaluation to ensure continuous improvement. Just because others call the company "world class" does not mean that the label is simply accepted as true. Scores on a recent follow-up self-evaluation were lower than on an initial one, primarily because employees have become increasingly self-critical and have acquired a better understanding of what is being measured. Continuous improvement is a never-ending journey. Incentives such as Eaton's own awards and the Malcolm Baldrige National Quality Award make the journey more exciting.

With an emphasis on listening to the customer, the company is seeking more ways to satisfy and anticipate customer needs. Having successfully initiated the procedure, it is working to further implement and institutionalize simultaneous engineering. Maintenance prevention is improving as design and manufacturing engineers work together to eliminate snags in early stages of the machine design and manufacturing processes. As equipment and its accompanying manuals become increasingly complex, training programs within the company become more sophisticated. The needs of both internal and external customers are of prime concern in all areas, including such simple tasks as housekeeping within the maintenance environment. The goal is to have a world-class "tour-ready" manufacturing department at all times.

Relationships with the community provide another area of growth and customer satisfaction for the company. Closer ties with local vocational schools can help develop a more highly skilled pool of new labor. All of this is essential to the Hydraulics Division because, according to manufacturing services manager David Bjork, "We intend to get better at what we are already good at." With such a commitment to continuous improvement, Eaton will remain a major competitor in the marketplace.

ARE THERE OTHERS?

In our research into what is happening in companies across the United States, we have been both encouraged and discouraged. We have learned that there are other companies like the ones previously cited. A select few are more willing than others to share specific statistics; among those are companies that are competing for major awards.

Part of the hesitation in providing data comes from the fact that it is almost impossible to obtain when there have been no previously established benchmarks. As companies become more involved in TPM, they have increasingly focused on the need for benchmarks, and vital data is slowly becoming more obtainable.

The most discouraging news is that some organizations have forgotten that the journey is never ending. After exerting tremendous energy to seed a strategy, they forget that like a newborn child, it needs continual attention. Any parent with grown children knows that working through the stages of childhood and adolescence does not end the relationship. It changes, but it is ongoing. Managers who do not realize this quickly undo all they originally accomplished. Support must remain visible, and it must be tangible. Too many companies that aspire to world-class status still respond to questions about their TPM strategy with, "Oh yes, we'd better do something about that." They may have begun to work on TPM, but have decided that it is too difficult, too costly, or not showy enough. They treat it as something that can be put on or taken off according to whim, like a change of clothing.

Only when TPM becomes so institutionalized that it is as natural as breathing can a company say that it has a world-class TPM strategy. To date, we have found that no company in the United States can say that. Some are further along the journey than others. They may be the first to arrive — if they don't get distracted along the way.

16

Consequences:
So What If We Don't Do It?

So what if we don't do it? Life goes on. Life may go on for some, but not for all. Manufacturing industries that have continued for many years have made massive changes to keep up with the changing needs of their customers. Those that have ignored customer requirements are no longer in business or have forfeited large chunks of their market share.

THE BOTTOM LINE

We have heard all kinds of arguments against adopting TPM. "It's too hard. We don't have time. Our people won't go along with it. It's too costly. It's a good idea, but we've got to get the numbers out first. We've never done it that way before. It's just a fad. We're making a profit without it. It's not necessary. We don't have the personnel. The bottom line is what counts." Our point is to convince you that TPM *is* the bottom line! It is the foundation for success.

Many people have recognized the importance of TPM over the years, but most have been the wrong people. The ones who need to know are the corporate leadership. We prefer to believe that they really don't know. The alternative is that they do know, but don't care. There may be a few who don't care, but we believe most leaders are concerned about the welfare of their companies.

THE ROLE OF GENERALS

The people most important to the success of TPM are a company's CEO, president, and vice presidents. Until top managers recognize the importance of TPM and visibly support it through active participation, maintenance will continue to be the stepchild of the organization.

We would not think of sending soldiers into battle without direction from their generals. The generals would not dream of sending pilots into combat if that aircraft lacked vital parts or had been improperly maintained. The generals are the ones who make the big decisions. They are responsible for the outcome of the tactics they employ, and they recognize that their success is dependent on the troops they command. Those leading our manufacturing organizations should be equally accountable for the way they lead their companies.

Senior management cannot give lip service to TPM and expect it to succeed. The commitment must be wholehearted and unwavering. Leaders at all levels of the organization must understand the value of TPM. Unfortunately, TPM is beyond the scope of some organizations whose leadership lacks the vision and the *dedication to purpose* required to institutionalize TPM strategies. They will go the way of the dinosaur.

Those who have the will can reap wonderful rewards, including achievement of world-class status. There are some major hurdles to overcome, though. CEOs and vice presidents must go with maintenance personnel to TPM seminars. Instead of telling employees to set up training within the organization, they must participate in the training. They must also be willing to pick up the paper on the floor, read Pareto charts, and ask employees about such matters as equipment operation, product quality, and training programs. They must be honest with employees about the seriousness of competition. They must work with their employees, not oversee them.

In addition to being tuned in to every facet of the organization, senior management must be prepared to make tough decisions. As a vintner extensively and carefully prunes the vines, so must senior management recognize dead or diseased wood within the organization and remove it before blight can spread.

SUSTAINING IMPROVEMENT

To sustain continuous improvement, a positive attitude throughout the company must be evident. An enthusiasm and enchantment with new ideas must permeate the atmosphere. Nurturing such an environment is the job of senior management. People must also be communicated with; they must feel appreciated and needed if they are to maintain the commitment required in a world-class organization. The leader who adds to an individual's responsibilities without explanation or changes a work assignment arbitrarily is not a leader but a dictator. Such a person does the company more harm than good.

One of the sad commentaries of our society is that the motivation most people now have for working is to support their leisure activities. They do not have a work ethic based on the satisfaction of a job well done. Yet the worker is not entirely to blame for this. If management and shareholders demand profits over all else, quality will be sacrificed. An individual forced to produce an inferior product has no pride in workmanship, and the ethic of quality disappears. Likewise, when workers are expected to produce quality without adequate resources and support, stress levels rise and burnout quickly follows.

ATTITUDES AND CONSEQUENCES

The most difficult aspect of implementing TPM is not in finding the dollars to support start-up costs but finding people with the positive attitudes needed to initiate and sustain change. Maintenance has been a subculture in most organizations for so long that most people are unaware of its importance, nor do they want to elevate it to the status it deserves. Employers may be willing to spend whatever is necessary to attract top engineers, but they still cut costs by hiring the least expensive rather than the best-trained technicians to maintain their equipment.

There are two results of this attitude. The most obvious is that designs may be good, but actually achieving production on schedule is almost impossible. The second difficulty is far more insidious. Because we denigrate maintenance and technical skill areas, our young people do not want to be associated with these areas. They prefer to train for careers offering more opportunity for advancement, reward, recognition, and respect for their skills. As a result, there is a shortage of technically skilled people in today's work force. We must look to other countries for such skilled individuals, while our own young people flock to more prestigious fields that are already overcrowded.

So what if TPM is not implemented? We will continue to encourage people to go into careers that offer hope for greater status but less chance of employment. We will continue to look to other countries to provide real skills while deluding ourselves that an information-based society does not really need mechanical or technical know-how. Our equipment will continue to become more antiquated and less efficient. Customers will look elsewhere for quality and on-time deliveries. We will admit, as some have suggested, that we are indeed a second-rate nation and concede our world markets to those willing to invest time, resources, and energy in developing them. We will ignore ISO 9000, world-class manufacturing, and other such strategies as we return to isolationist views and let others assume leadership roles in the world.

So what if we don't adopt TPM and move into world-class competition? Someone else will. They will reap the benefits when we are no longer around. Only time can provide the answer to this question: *Is the tiger really waking up or simply stretching in its sleep?*

17

Action Plan: Entering the TPM Race

We have deliberately avoided writing a technical manual about the nuts and bolts of implementing TPM because this has already been done by people knowledgeable in their fields. Once the need for a life preserver is understood, it becomes a simple matter to teach an individual how to use it properly. The most concise, easily understood directions are of little use, however, to those who are convinced that knowing how to swim is enough to prevent drowning.

We sincerely hope we have convinced you that a life preserver is essential and that you are now ready to delve into the instruction manuals for preserving your business. If you are determined to enter the race, you must be equally determined to finish it. Many detours will tempt you along the way. If you shift your focus, you may win one heat, but lose the race. TPM is not a dash, but a marathon that demands concentrated attention and dedication.

IMPROVING PRODUCTIVITY

Dr. Ken Hoyt, University Distinguished Professor of Education at Kansas State University and former director of the U.S.

Office of Career Education, has conceptualized the need for educational reform by viewing the classroom as a "workplace"
and both the pupil and the teacher as "workers." In doing so, he
has collated a number of suggested changes for improving productivity used in various industries and suggested that, with
slight adaptations, they can be used to improve productivity in
the education system. We think his seven basic ways of improving can be applied to a wide variety of settings. The example
used here is attempt to apply these seven ways of improving
productivity to TPM in the manufacturing environment. They
can obviously be applied to many other environments.

Workers need to be shown the importance of a task. Employees who know that reducing costs is directly related to the
size of the paycheck will be more concerned about their performance level than those who do not see the correlation. We need
to teach our workers (and our children) that there will be *no* jobs
unless the company is profitable.

An individual working in a bolt factory may have little
idea of where the product will be used, whether in a washing
machine or an aircraft engine. If everyone performed their tasks
as if they were essential to the safety of a plane they might be
flying on tomorrow, it would be astounding how rapidly quality
and productivity would improve. Our space program has
proved that we are capable of producing at the highest standards in the world when workers understand the importance of
what they are doing. When we denigrate any task or sacrifice
quality for expediency at any point, we risk tragedy, as the
Challenger disaster so painfully reminds us.

Efforts should be rewarded when they occur. Immediate
positive feedback ensures that the effort will be repeated. If this
can be followed up with a substantial longer-term reward, such
as a bonus or profit-sharing opportunities, that is even better.
Delaying the reward too long, however, will negate its value.

Tight budgets are no excuse for failure to recognize effort. A "thank you," "good job," or "Joe figured it out!" costs nothing, but provides support through awareness and sensitivity. Articles in company newsletters, pictures or posters on bulletin boards, or features in local newspapers or trade journals require an investment in time rather than money and can be even more meaningful.

Empower your workers to the extent that they are willing to accept responsibility for their actions. Those who feel uncomfortable with new responsibilities should not be forced to take them on. Those who like challenge should be given the opportunity to participate at a level commensurate with the responsibility they are capable of assuming. Unfortunately, some want the power but not the responsibility. They should be given neither.

Introduce variety into your workplace. Variety increases learning and skill levels while it reduces boredom. Job rotation, multiskilling, training, and an opportunity to view the entire manufacturing process are some ways to introduce variety. In other instances, it may need to be addressed in an approach unique to the particular industry.

This kind of variety may prove to be a challenge in organizations that have strict job descriptions. We need to rethink the ways we assign tasks so that workers are given jobs with recognizable outcomes. When the finished product is never seen, whether it is a subassembly or final goods, it is difficult to feel responsible for its quality. Understanding the importance of the part without knowing how it fits with the whole is also difficult.

Encourage teamwork and shared responsibility for implementing TPM. It is impossible for one or two people to support a major change through the initiation stage. Sharing responsibility results in shared ownership. The more people with a vested interest in the outcome, the greater your chances of achieving the goal.

Recognize and reward productive work habits wherever they occur. TPM is an interrelated strategy and should be treated as such. When people with no direct interest in TPM are recognized for contributing to the strategy, they become more interested in it. The naturally neat and clean individual who keeps equipment spotless for personal satisfaction should be recognized as a TPM supporter. When workers realize that TPM changes the way they work instead of making more work, they will be more willing to move away from the comfort zone of the status quo.

Resources

Although the body of literature relating to TPM is growing, relatively few books are available on the topic. These are sufficient, however, to meet the needs of any company truly interested in implementing the strategy.

Books that provide foundational understanding for world-class manufacturing include Richard J. Schonberger's *Japanese Manufacturing Techniques: Nine Hidden Lessons in Simplicity* (New York: Free Press, 1982) and *World-Class Manufacturing: The Lessons of Simplicity Applied* (New York: Free Press, 1986). Peter C. Reid's *Well Made in America* (New York: McGraw-Hill, 1990) is a case study of Harley-Davidson's attempts to survive global competition. Ira Magaziner's books, *Minding America's Business: The Decline and Rise of American Economy* (New York: Harcourt Brace Jovanovich, 1982) (coauthored by Robert B. Reich), and *The Silent War: Inside the Global Business Battles Shaping America's Future* (New York: Random House, 1989) (coauthored by Mark Patinkin), provide numerous insights and case studies, as does Seymour Melman's *Profits without Production* (New York: Knopf, 1983). Tom Peters's *Thriving on Chaos* (New York: Harper & Row, 1987), as well as Michael Dertouzos, et al., *Made in America*

(Cambridge: MIT Press, 1987), Schonberger's *Building a Chain of Customers* (New York: Free Press, 1990), and Kenichi Ohmae's *The Mind of the Strategist: The Art of Japanese Business* (New York: McGraw-Hill, 1982), are also helpful in understanding the intricacies of today's international manufacturing environment. These books are not particularly technical and make relatively easy reading.

The classics of TPM implementation are undoubtedly the works edited by Seiichi Nakajima: *Introduction to TPM: Total Productive Maintenance* (Cambridge: Productivity Press, 1988) and *TPM Development Program: Implementing Total Productive Maintenance* (Cambridge: Productivity Press, 1989). These books are the foundation for any TPM library. Kunio Shirose's *TPM for Workshop Leaders* (Cambridge: Productivity Press, 1992) collects and condenses the main points of TPM in a form accessible to supervisors and other shop-floor leaders. Masaaki Imai's *Kaizen: The Key to Japan's Competitive Success* (New York: McGraw-Hill, 1986) provides helpful statistical documentation to support the use of TPM. Keith Mobley's *Introduction to Predictive Maintenance* (New York: Van Nostrand Reinhold, 1990) is a thorough resource on this component of TPM, while Terry Wireman's *World-Class Maintenance Management* (New York: Industrial Press, 1990) deals with managing maintenance functions and organizations.

Training For TPM: A Manufacturing Success Story (Cambridge: Productivity Press, 1990), edited by Nachi-Fujikoshi Corporation, is an in-depth case study of a Japanese PM–Prize-winning company that is unique in its commitment to improving the skill levels of all employees, its companywide quality organization supporting TPM, and its internal use of much of the equipment it produces.

Roy L. Harmon and Leroy D. Peterson have written in depth, in a very readable style, about organizing focused factories. Their book, *Reinventing the Factory* (New York: Free Press, 1990), also touches on world-class strategies in relation to this organizational framework. *Just-In-Time Purchasing* by A. Ansari and B. Modarress (New York: Free Press, 1990) deals with purchasing in a just-in-time environment, including such topics as costs and transportation systems, implementation, and quality control. Since TPM is a support for the other world-class manufacturing strategies, these are also worthy of scrutiny.

In addition to the books available, we have found a growing number of valuable articles in magazines and trade journals. *Business Week, Engineer's Digest, Fortune, Industrial Engineering, Industry Week, Maintenance Technology, Plant Engineering, Plant Services,* and *P/PM Technology* are among those we have found useful. Newsletters like TPM, published by the American Institute for Total Productive Maintenance, are also helpful.

Understanding of TPM can be improved through attending a variety of seminars and workshops that focus on the topic. These are valuable in terms of both technical learning and the practical experiences of others. Productivity, Inc., of Cambridge, MA., has been a leader in TPM, providing workshops, newsletters, books, and training events. It sponsored the first TPM conference in the United States, which has become an annual fall event, and organized the American Institute for Total Productive Maintenance. These are excellent resources for those who wish to expand their network of those involved with the development of TPM strategy.

If a company's greatest danger is that no one bothers to learn about TPM, the second-greatest danger is that those who are aware of TPM try to learn all there is to know before doing anything. True learning takes place only with active involvement. Quickly developing a basic understanding of TPM and sharing that understanding with others in your organization will enhance your chances of competing successfully in the twenty-first century.

Glossary

Autonomous maintenance: Component of TPM that involves production machine operators in the total equipment maintenance process.

Bottleneck: A resource that, because of its capabilities or limitations, governs throughput and inventory.

Computerized maintenance management system (CMMS): Computerized system for managing preventive maintenance and equipment parts inventory.

Corrective maintenance: Component of TPM related to equipment modification to improve performance of existing equipment or by adapting new equipment to the manufacturing environment.

Deming management method: A management system developed by W.E. Deming emphasizing the need for employee involvement and continued interaction among research and development, production, and sales to improve quality and satisfy customers.

Flexible manufacturing system: Flexible computer-controlled equipment that is capable of handling rapidly changing product designs and production of small lot sizes.

Implementation: The second stage of the change process, which becomes operative after pilot projects have proved their worth and are adopted as standard procedure.

Initialization: The first stage of the change process, which involves selling others on an idea. It may also be referred to as initiation.

Institutionalization: The final stage of the change process, in which the change has become an accepted part of the modus operandi.

ISO 9000: A series of new international standards for quality of processes.

Just-in-time (JIT): A strategy of production and inventory control that reduces waste by producing goods only in quantities sold.

Local performance measurement: A system for measuring performance at each step of the manufacturing process.

Maintenance prevention: Component of TPM in which equipment is designed or selected for reliability and ease of maintenance.

Operating expense: Money spent to turn inventory into throughput.

Predictive maintenance: Component of TPM that collects data to determine the life expectancy of components in order to replace or service them at the optimum time to avoid unscheduled downtime.

Preventive maintenance (PM): Component of TPM in which equipment maintenance is done on a scheduled basis to reduce machine breakdowns and malfunctions and ensure the continuous, smooth operation of equipment.

Statistical process control (SPC): A system using control charts for capturing problem data by focusing on one or more critical factors in the manufacturing process and using them to determine when to stop the process. Also known as statistical quality control (SQC) and statistical quality management (SQM).

Throughput: Rate at which an organization generates money through the sale of its products.

Total employee involvement (TEI): Involvement of all employees at all levels, in the continual improvement of products, processes and systems necessary to become and remain world class. Also referred to as employee involvement (EI).

Total productive maintenance (TPM): A system for designing or selecting, correcting, and maintaining equipment so that breakdowns and malfunctions rarely occur during production runs.

Total quality control (TQC): The organization of activities so that everyone is involved in a totally integrated effort to improve performance at every level, resulting in only quality goods proceeding through the manufacturing process. Also known as total quality management (TQM).

Work-in-process (WIP): Material in the process of being converted into saleable goods.

World-class manufacturing (WCM): An operational strategy of continuous improvement, powered by the synergy of the interconnected elements of total quality management, just-in-time, total employee involvement, and total productive maintenance, which promotes the production of quality goods at a minimum cost while meeting or exceeding customer expectations, thereby enabling the organization to compete effectively in world markets.

Notes

CHAPTER ONE

1. R. Keith Mobley, "Maintenance in the 1990s," *Engineer's Digest* (Jan. 1990, 26).

CHAPTER TWO

1. Michael Fullan, *The Meaning of Educational Change* (New York: Teachers College, Columbia University, 1982), 163-169.

CHAPTER THREE

1. A. Groner, *The American Heritage History of American Business & Industry* (New York: American Heritage Publishing, 1972).

2. Seymour Melman, *Profits without Production* (New York: Knopf, 1983), 6.

3. Robert H. Hayes and Steven C. Wheelwright, *Restoring Our Competitive Edge: Competing Through Manufacturing* (New York: Wiley, 1984), 10.

4. According to productivity expert Seymour Melman, short-term profits are more attractive than reinvestment for five reasons:

1. They are less subject to the pressures of inflation.
2. They are less affected by the fluctuating values of currency.
3. The cost of investment capital, which is in short supply, is high.
4. Government has a dual influence on profits, through the tax system as well as through its role as a major contractor.
5. Bonuses for senior managers are tied directly to current profits. Melman, op. cit., 40-69.

5. Ibid, 10.

6. Eliyahu M. Goldratt and Robert E. Fox, *The Race* (Croton-on-Hudson, NY: North River Press, 1986), 8.

CHAPTER FOUR

1. Thomas G. Gunn, *Computer Applications In Manufacturing* (New York: Industrial Press, 1981), 182.

2. Robert H. Hayes and Steven C. Wheelwright, *Restoring Our Competitive Edge: Competing Through Manufacturing* (New York: Wiley, 1984), 338.

3. Tom Peters, *Thriving on Chaos* (New York: Harper & Row, 1987), 81.

4. Lester C. Thurow, "A Weakness in Process Technology" *Science*, 238 (Dec. 18, 1987), 1659-1662.

5. Ira Magaziner and Mark Patinkin, *The Silent War: Inside the Global Business Battles Shaping America's Future* (New York: Random House, 1989), 25-28, 285-299.

6. Mary Walton, *The Deming Management Method* (New York: Dodd, Mead, 1986).

7. Kenichi Ohmae, *The Mind of the Strategist: The Art of Japanese Business* (New York: McGraw-Hill, 1982), 243.

8. Rodney Clark, *The Japanese Company* (New Haven: Yale University Press, 1979), 174-179.

9. Vaughn Beals, "Harley-Davidson: An American Success Story," *Journal for Quality and Participation*, 11-2, June 1988, A19-A23.

10. Richard J. Schonberger, *Japanese Manufacturing Techniques: Nine Hidden Lessons in Simplicity* (New York: Free Press, 1982), 66, 136-137.

11. Richard J. Schonberger, *World Class Manufacturing: The Lessons of Simplicity Applied* (New York: Free Press, 1986), 7.

12. Ibid, 75.

CHAPTER FIVE

1. Masaaki Imai, *Kaizen: The Key to Japan's Competitive Success* (New York: McGraw-Hill, 1986), 159.

2. R. T. Lubben, *Just-In-Time Manufacturing: An Aggressive Manufacturing Strategy* (New York: McGraw-Hill, 1986), 148.

3. Charles Garfield, *Peak Performers: The New Heroes of American Business* (New York: William Morrow, 1986), 128-129, quoting Rene McPherson, Stanford Graduate School of Business.

4. Imai, op. cit., 158-161.

5. Peter C. Reid, *Well-Made in America: Lessons from Harley-Davidson on Being the Best* (New York: McGraw-Hill, 1990), 159-163.

6. Schonberger (1986) op. cit., 65-72.

7. Ibid, 70.

8. Eliyahu Goldratt and Robert E. Fox, *The Race* (Croton-on-Hudson, NY: North River Press, 1986), 149.

9. *Productivity* newsletter, 9:6 (June 1989), 6.

10. R. Keith Mobley, "Maintenance in the 1990s," *Engineer's Digest*, (Jan. 1990), 30.

CHAPTER SIX

1. This research was undertaken in September, 1988 as part of a thesis requirement for Herbert Steinbacher at Colorado Christian University. TPM was selected as a topic at a time when Mr. Steinbacher's employer, Teledyne Water Pik, was beginning to adopt just-in-time and Deming management approaches, but little information was available about TPM as a complementary strategy. The questionnaire was developed to provide identifying data as a basis for comparison, with open-ended questions about the benefits and problems seen by facilities/maintenance managers within the companies interviewed.

The research sample was chosen to compare Colorado companies with those in other areas of the country that were pursuing world-class manufacturing strategies. The national companies were selected from Schonberger's appendix to *World Class Manufacturing* entitled "Honor Roll: The 5-10-20s," which lists companies showing a fivefold or better gain in productivity, primarily based on JIT-related improvements. This group was selected for reasons of expediency such as ease of identification, similarity, and world class-involvement.

The Colorado list was selected from companies included in the *Directory of Colorado Manufacturers* (Boulder: Business Research Division, University of Colorado, 1988) that reported a work force of at least 250 people, although some of the data received indicated that the companies were in fact smaller. Colorado companies that appeared on Schonberger's list elected not to participate, so there was no overlap between the two sample groups.

2. Richard J. Schonberger, *World Class Manufacturing: The Lessons of Simplicity Applied* (New York: Free Press, 1986), 228-236.

3. R. Keith Mobley, *An Introduction to Predictive Maintenance* (New York: Van Nostrand Reinhold, 1990), 13.

4. "Maintenance Today: State of the Art or Wishful Thinking," *Plant Engineering* (April 12, 1990), D2-D7.

5. R. J. Schonberger, op. cit., 7.

6. R. K. Mobley, op. cit., 3.

7. Tom Stevens, "Continuous Improvement in Maintenance," *Maintenance Technology*, Vol.3, No. 4 (April 1990), 31-34.

8. "Wear Particle Analysis . . . An Integral Part of Machine Condition Monitoring at American Cyanamid's Westwego, LA Plant," *P/PM Technology*, 3:3 (May/June, 1990), 27-28.

9. Ira Magaziner and Mark Patinkin, *The Silent War: Inside the Global Business Battles Shaping America's Future* (New York: Random House, 1989), 94.

10. H. R. Steinbacher, thesis study on total productive maintenance for Colorado Christian University (Denver, 1989).

11. Edgar H. Schein, *Organizational Psychology*, 3rd ed. (Englewood Cliffs, NJ: Prentice-Hall, 1980).

12. Tom Peters, *Thriving on Chaos* (New York: Harper & Row, 1987), 112.

13. J. Roe, "Determining Financial Benefits For Predictive Maintenance and Developing Management Support," *P/PM Technology*, 3:3 (May/June, 1990), 18- 20.

14. "Maintenance Today," op. cit.

15. H. T. Amrine, J. A. Ritchey, and C. L. Moodie, *Manufacturing Organization and Management* (Englewood Cliffs, NJ: Prentice-Hall, 1987).

16. S. Macaulay, "Amazing Things Can Happen If You . . . 'Keep It Clean'" *Production*, Vol.100, No. 5 (May 19, 1988), 72-74.

CHAPTER EIGHT

1. "TPM: More Than Theory for Two Manufacturers," *Industrial Maintenance & Plant Operation*, 51:9 (Sept. 1990), 48.

2. Michael L. Dertouzos, et al., *Made In America: Regaining the Productive Edge* (Cambridge: MIT Press, 1989), 45.

CHAPTER THIRTEEN

1. "The Forgotten Half," *U.S. News & World Report* (June 26, 1989), 46-53.

About the Authors

Herbert R. Steinbacher has been an advocate of TPM throughout his working career. He has recognized the importance of maintenance since working as a mechanic in the U.S. Air Force, where he was also an aircraft engines instructor and airborne avionics superintendent. He received a Bronze Star for service for his contributions as an adviser to the Vietnamese Air Force.

Mr. Steinbacher has worked for Storage Technology and currently is employed with Teledyne Water Pik; his positions have included administrator of contract services and manager of maintenance and facilities. He holds a B.S. in management of human resources from Colorado Christian University and has spoken at several conferences, including the first TPM conference in the United States.

Mr. Steinbacher is a charter member of the American Institute for Total Productive Maintenance and the International Facilities Management Association. He also serves as a TPM consultant on request.

Norma L. Steinbacher is a counselor with the Longmont, Colorado public schools. Her long-standing involvement in career education has brought her in contact with a wide variety of businesses and industries. She was instrumental in the development of a job-shadowing program for students and a district-wide career education program. She currently serves on the Longmont Chamber of Commerce Education Committee.

Ms. Steinbacher holds a B.A. in history and psychology from Taylor University and an M.A. in guidance and counseling from Michigan State University. She has also done graduate work at the University of Colorado, Colorado State University, and the University of Northern Colorado. She is a member of the American Association for Counseling and Development, American School Counselors Association, National Association for Counseling and Development, Colorado Association for Counseling and Development, Colorado School Counselors Association, Colorado Career Development Association, and St. Vrain Valley Counselors.

Through her work in Michigan, North Carolina, and Colorado, Ms. Steinbacher has developed insights regarding the successes, difficulties, and needs of American industry. She is a strong supporter of industry-education partnerships and recognizes the importance of addressing the change process in business as well as in education.

Index

-A-

Allen-Bradley Co., Inc., 28,
    111-14
American Cyanamid, 40
Amrine, Harold, 42
Autonomous maintenance
    definition of, 4, 25, 29
    importance of, 29-31, 97-99
    training and, 99-101

-B-

Beals, Vaughn, 21, 111
Bjork, David, 115

-C-

Change/change process
    emotional aspect of, 51

human component of, 11-12
implementing, 11, 60-65
importance of, 6-7, 9
incentives for, 10
initiating, 10-11, 59-60
institutionalization, 10,
    65-66
personalities and, 47-49
recognizing the need for,
    49-51
stages in, 10, 59-66
training/education and,
    51-57
Computerized maintenance
    management
    system (CMMS), 61, 86
Corning, 20
Corrective maintenance
    definition of, 3, 25, 27

Corrective maintenance *(cont.)*
  difference between predic-
    tive maintenance and, 87
  examples of, 90-91
  hidden maintenance costs,
    89-90
  importance of, 27-29, 91
  reasons for modifications,
    87-89
Customer satisfaction
  competition and, 10
  TPM and, 41

-D-

Data collection, 80-82, 95
Deming, W. E., 21
*Directory of Colorado Manu-
  facturers*, 36
Downtime, eliminating
  machine, 39-40

-E-

Eaton Corp., 114-15
Eddy current testing, 85
Education. *See* Training
Employee attitudes, 40-41
  as internal customers, 41-42
Employee involvement
  data collection and, 81-82
  maintenance prevention
    and, 74-75
  total, 23, 74-75
Equipment manufacturers,
  role of, 75-78

-F-

Fullan, Michael, 10

-G-

General Electric (GE), 14, 20,
  49-50
General Motors Corp. (GM),
  15
Gunn, Thomas, 19

-H-

Harley-Davidson, Inc., 21, 29,
  33, 49, 101, 110-11
Hayes, Robert, 16, 19
Hoyt, Ken, 123-24
Human component of TPM,
  11-12

-I-

Imai, Masaaki, 25
Implementation stage of
  change, 11, 60-65
Initiation stage of change,
  10-11, 59-60
Institutionalization stage of
  change, 10, 65-66
Introduction to TPM
  (Nakajima), 13
ISO 9000, 108

-J-

Just-in-time (JIT), 22-23, 106

-L-

Life-cycle costing, 36, 43
Lifetime employment, 21
Local performance measurements, 31
Lubben, Richard, 26
Lubrication analysis, 84-85

-M-

Magaziner, Ira, 40
Maintenance prevention
  benefits of, 71-72
  costs and, 26
  definition of, 3, 25
  employee involvement and, 74-75
  importance of implementing at the design stage, 67-71
  practicality and realism in design, 72-74
  role of equipment manufacturer in, 75-78
Management, role of, 21, 118-19
Manufacturing industry
  changes in, 4-5
  historical background of, 14-17
Massachusetts Institute of Technology (MIT), 17
  Commission on Industrial Productivity, 66

Mobley, Keith, 34, 38
Moody, C. L., 42

-N-

Nakajima, Seiichi, 13
NASA, 90
National Award for Maintenance Management Excellence, 13
Nissan, 42

-P-

Patinkin, Mark, 40
Peters, Tom, 20
Plant Engineering, 42
Predictive maintenance, 79
  cost savings and, 82-83, 85-86
  data collection and, 80-82
  definition of, 3, 25, 26
  difference between corrective maintenance and, 87
  importance of, 26-27
  methods for measuring machine conditions, 83-85
Preventive maintenance
  data collection and, 95
  definition of, 3, 25
  importance of, 24, 29, 93-95
Productivity, methods for improving, 123-26

-Q-

Quality
  control, importance of, 22
  cost of, 5-6
Quigley, Ron L., xx, 113, 114

-R-

Recognition/rewards, 62,
  124-25, 126
Ritchey, J. A., 42
Roe, John, 42

-S-

Schein, Edgar, 41
Schonberger, Richard, 13, 22,
  24, 33, 36, 39
Snyder, Miles, 76
Statistical process analysis,
  80-82
Stevens, Tom, 39
Swisher, Jerry, 76

-T-

Technical Assistance Research
  Programs, Inc., 41
TechniStar Corp., 75-78
Teerlink, Richard, 111
Temperature measurements,
  85
Tennessee Eastman, 60-61
Thurow, Lester, 20
Topy Industries' Ayase Works,
  32

Total employee involvement,
  23, 74-75
Total productive maintenance
  (TPM)
  benefits of, 32-33, 35, 37-38,
    39-44
  as a component of WCM, 24
  components of, 3-4, 25
  consequences of not imple-
    menting, 120-21
  costs of, 26
  defining, 25-34
  disadvantages of, 31-32,
    38-39
  historical background of,
    13-17
  human component of, 11-12
  implementing, 33-34, 38-39
  importance of, 6-7, 36-37
Total quality management, 23
TPM: Development Program
  (Nakajima), 13
Training
  autonomous maintenance
    and, 99-101
  challenge of future, 53-55
  change and continuing
    education, 51-53
  cost versus savings, 85-86
  job abuse eliminated with,
    55-56
  necessity of, 56-57
Training for TPM
  (Nachi-Fujikoshi), 13

-V-

Value-added operations, 23, 33
Vaughn, Wayne, 111
Vibration analysis, 84

-W-

Wheelwright, Steven, 16, 19
Whitney, Eli, 14
World-class manufacturing
        (WCM),
    components of, 22-24
World Class Manufacturing
        (Schonberger), 13

OTHER PRODUCTS ON
TOTAL PRODUCTIVE MAINTENANCE (TPM)

Productivity Press publishes and distributes materials on continuous improvement in productivity, quality, and the creative involvement of all employees. Many of our products are direct source materials from Japan that have been translated into English for the first time and are available exclusively from Productivity. Supplemental products and services include membership groups, conferences, seminars, in-house training and consulting, audio-visual training programs, and industrial study missions. Call toll-free 1-800-394-6868 for our free catalog.

Introduction to TPM
Total Productive Maintenance

Seiichi Nakajima

Total Productive Maintenance (TPM) combines preventive maintenance with Japanese concepts of total quality control (TQC) and total employee involvement (TEI). The result is a new system for equipment maintenance that optimizes effectiveness, eliminates breakdowns, and promotes autonomous operator maintenance through day-to-day activities. Here are the steps involved in TPM and case examples from top Japanese plants.
ISBN 0-915299-23-2 / 149 pages / $45.00 / Order ITPM-B227

Total Productive Maintenance
Maximizing Productivity and Quality (AV)

Japan Management Association (ed.)

Introduce TPM to your work force with this accessible two-part audio visual program, which explains the rationale and basic principles of TPM to supervisors, group leaders, and workers. It explains five major developmental activities of TPM, includes a section on equipment improvement that focuses on eliminating chronic losses, and describes an analytical approach called PM Analysis to help solve problems that have complex and continuously changing causes. (Approximately 45 minutes long.)
ISBN 0-915299-49-6 / 2 videos / $799.00 / Order VTPM-B227

Productivity Press, Inc., Dept. BK, P.O. Box 3007, Cambridge, MA 02140 1-800-274-9911

Training for TPM
A Manufacturing Success Story
Nachi-Fujikoshi (ed.)

A detailed case study of TPM implementation at a world-class manufacturer of bearings, precision machine tools, dies, industrial equipment, and robots. In just 22 years the company was awarded Japan's prestigious PM Prize for its program. Here's a detailed account of their improvement activities—and an impressive model for yours.
ISBN 0-915299-34-8 / 272 pages / $65.00 / Order CTPM-B227

TPM Development Program
Implementing Total Productive Maintenance
Seiichi Nakajima (ed.)

This book outlines a three-year program for systematic TPM development and implementation. It describes in detail the five principal developmental activities of TPM:

- Systematic elimination of the six big equipment related losses through small group activities
- Autonomous maintenance (by operators)
- Scheduled maintenance for the maintenance department
- Training in operation and maintenance skills
- Comprehensive equipment management from the design stage

ISBN 0-915299-37-2 / 428 pages / $85.00 / Order DTPM-B227

Equipment Planning for TPM
Maintenance Prevention Design
Fumio Gotoh

This practical book for design engineers, maintenance technicians, and manufacturing managers details a systematic approach to the improvement of equipment development and design and product manufacturing. The author analyzes five basic conditions for factory equipment of the future: development, reliability, economics, availability, and maintainability. The book's revolutionary concepts of equipment design and development enables managers to reduce equipment development time, balance maintenance and equipment planning and improvement, and improve quality production equipment.
ISBN 0-915299-77-1 / 320 pages / $85.00 / Order ETPM-B227

Productivity Press, Inc., Dept. BK, P.O. Box 3007, Cambridge, MA 02140 1-800-274-9911

Eliminating Minor Stoppages on Automated Lines

Kikuo Suehiro

Stoppages of automated equipment lines severely affect productivity, cost, and lead time. Such losses make decreasing the number of stoppages a crucial element of TPM. Kikuo Suehiro has helped companies such as Hitachi achieve unprecedented reduction in the number of minor stoppages. In this explicitly detailed book, he presents a scientific approach to determining the causes of stoppages and the actions that can be taken to diminish their occurrence.
ISBN 1-56327-70-4 / 208 pages / $49.95 / Order ELIM-B227

TPM for Workshop Leaders

Kunio Shirose

A top TPM consultant in Japan, Kunio Shirose describes the problems that TPM group leaders are likely to experience and the improvements in quality and vast cost savings you should expect to achieve. In this non-technical overview of TPM, he incorporates cartoons and graphics to convey the hands-on leadership issues of TPM implementation. Case studies and realistic examples reinforce Shirose's ideas on training and managing equipment operators in the care of their equipment.
ISBN 0-915299-92-5 / 192 pages / $34.95 / Order TPMWSL-B227

New Directions for Total Productive Maintenance

Tokutaro Suzuki

This is the first book to examine the multitude of possibilities for TPM (Total Productive Maintenance) beyond the realm of repetitive manufacturing. Suzuki, Vice Chairman of the Japan Institute of Plant Maintenance, examines four major shifts in the direction of TPM application:

• The increasingly effective use of TPM in process industries

• The acceleration of TPM implementation in original equipment manufacturing

• The spread of TPM to departments other than production and maintenance, including administration, research and development, and sales

• The proliferation of TPM activities in companies outside Japan
ISBN 1-56327-011-0 / 303 pages / $59.95 / Order NDTPM-B227

20 Keys to Workplace Improvement

Iwao Kobayashi

This easy-to-read introduction to the "20 keys" system presents an integrated approach to assessing and improving your company's competitive level. The book focuses on systematic improvement through five levels of achievement in such primary areas as industrial housekeeping, small group activities, quick changeover techniques, equipment maintenance, and computerization. A scoring guide is included, along with information to help plan a strategy for your company's world class improvement effort.

ISBN 0-915299-61-5 / 264 pages / $29.95 / Order 20KEYS-B227

Productivity Press, Inc., Dept. BK, P.O. Box 3007, Cambridge, MA 02140 1-800-274-9911

JOIN THE AMERICAN INSTITUTE FOR TOTAL PRODUCTIVE MAINTENANCE (AITPM)

Maintenance costs make up between 15-40% of all manufacturing costs. TPM ensures lower maintenance costs by improving equipment reliability. The concept has been used in Japan for years and has just recently been introduced in America. The AITPM is your complete resource for learning how companies are using TPM to eliminate machine breakdowns, increase equipment effectiveness, and improve equipment design so machines don't break down in the first place. Membership benefits include a monthly newsletter, networking opportunities, conferences, and special discounts on selected books and events. To sign up, or for more information about this item only, call 1-800-394-5772.

TO ORDER: Write, phone, or fax Productivity Press, Dept. BK, P.O. Box 3007, Cambridge, MA 02140, phone 1-800-394-6868, fax 1-617-864-6286. Send check or charge to your credit card (American Express, Visa, MasterCard accepted).

U.S. ORDERS: Add $5 shipping for first book, $2 each additional for UPS surface delivery. Add $5 for each AV program containing 1 or 2 tapes; add $12 for each AV program containing 3 ore more tapes. CT residents add 6% and MA residents add 5% for sales tax. We offer attractive quantity discounts for bulk purchases of individual titles; call for more information

INTERNATIONAL ORDERS: Write, phone, or fax for quote and indicate shipping method desired. Prepayment in U.S. dollars must accompany your order (checks must be drawn on U.S. banks). When quote is returned with payment, your order will be shipped promptly by the method requested.

NOTE: Prices are in U.S. dollars and are subject to change without notice.